START-UPS AND
THE MOBILIZATION OF
SOCIAL INTERACTIONS

"The world is suffering from a range of political and financial crises and organizations today fresh ideas to help them rethink social and institutional change. In response, many companies are moving to a purpose-driven model. This book is an unprecedented rallying cry for change that builds on over three decades' worth of research and business ingenuity into the idea that business needs to operate with genuine purpose and community. *Start-ups and the Mobilization of Social Interactions* isn't just for entrepreneurs, either. It is for everyone who wants to understand how to build a new way to do business that harnesses the power of social connectedness, community and the spirit of activism. Everyone who is excited about the positive possibilities of enterprise should read this book!"

Robert V. Kozinets
Professor, University of Southern California, USA

"With this volume, the three authors offer an approach that combines the development of a social movement and the emergence of an entrepreneurial project. The book offers an interesting and original key for understanding this combination that has not yet been sufficiently investigated, but is rich in implications for today's world. It also highlights the close relationship between consumption and entrepreneurship phenomena which are addressed separately in traditional management approaches but that are today increasingly connected."

Simone Guercini
Professor, University of Florence, Italy

"Based on extensive research, this book's authors share a clear and simple approach to enable success in high-impact projects. This is an inspiring read for entrepreneurs and allies – coaches, consultants mentors – alike."

Dafna Kariv
Professor, Adelson School of Entrepreneurship,
Reichman University, Israel

START-UPS AND THE MOBILIZATION OF SOCIAL INTERACTIONS

BY

FRANCK BARÈS
HEC Montreal, Canada

BERNARD COVA
Kedge Business School, France

AND

ANICET NEMANI
BIMSTR, Cameroon

United Kingdom – North America – Japan – India
Malaysia – China

Emerald Publishing Limited
Howard House, Wagon Lane, Bingley BD16 1WA, UK

First edition 2023

Reprints and permissions service
Contact: permissions@emeraldinsight.com

British Library Cataloguing in Publication Data
A catalogue record for this book is available from the British Library

ISBN: 978-1-80455-609-2 (Print)
ISBN: 978-1-80455-606-1 (Online)
ISBN: 978-1-80455-608-5 (Epub)

ISOQAR certified
Management System,
awarded to Emerald
for adherence to
Environmental
standard
ISO 14001:2004.

ISOQAR
REGISTERED
Certificate Number 1985
ISO 14001

INVESTOR IN PEOPLE

CONTENTS

Contents vii

LIST OF FIGURE AND TABLE

FIGURE

TABLE

INTRODUCTION

In view of the environmental problems threatening the planet, the crisis of weakening social ties that has only deepened during the pandemic, and the more and more glaring limitations of the capitalist system, we believe it is important to present an alternative to the standard model of business creation. The one we propose in this book makes community – understood as a social phenomenon that emerges and develops to support a movement and defend a cause – the basis of all initiative.

What led us to this alternative? We want to take advantage of this introduction to reveal what took place behind the scenes while we were writing the book you are about to read. We hope that what we have to say in these few lines will help you decide on the legitimacy and the relevance of the position that we put forward in this book.

The book began as a creative encounter between three men and three continents.

In 2017, Bernard Cova, a professor in the Department of Marketing and New Consumption at the Kedge Business School in Marseille, France, spent four months with the Department of Entrepreneurship and Innovation at HEC Montréal in Québec, Canada, where he pursued his research on brand communities. While there, he met Franck Barès, a professor of entrepreneurship who is also from France and who specializes in entrepreneurial support. The two compatriots developed a friendship and quickly decided to collaborate on research centring around the passion that entrepreneurs share with their communities.

A year later, Bernard and Franck created a training seminar for Executive Education HEC Montréal that was called *Supporting Passionate Entrepreneurs*, which they then adapted for a series of workshops that they gave to entrepreneurs in the Kedge Business School incubation programme. At the end of a workshop in Marseille, one of the participants walked straight up to them and said,

'Professors, everything you've presented today is in line with how I live my life – my adventure!' This was how Anicet Nemani entered the lives of the two professors. Living in France and having a passion for music from his home country of Cameroon, Anicet had founded BIMSTR, a music platform dedicated to the emergence of new Cameroonian talent. After the initial encounter with Bernard and Franck at the workshop, there followed an exchange at the Kedge cafeteria, a few discussions over lunch, finally some work sessions – and the trio had come to be!

Together they compared the theories on entrepreneurship and on the management of brand communities with the reality of an entrepreneurial journey that has important communitarian dimensions. Using their knowledge and expertise, the two professors could decode the entrepreneurial behaviour of Anicet who, reaping the benefits of their advice, adopted an economically viable business plan to further develop his community project to defend Cameroonian music and emerging musical talent. From these exchanges there came forth a credo: 'First community, second start-up'. This was how the idea for *Start-ups and the Mobilization of Social Interactions* was born.

This book is also a message that the authors have for management and entrepreneurship experts all around the world. Beyond the myth of the start-up nation, hypergrowth and speculation on future business value, there exists an alternative form of entrepreneurship that needs the support of young entrepreneurs and that should be fostered among them. We call it 'entrepreneurial activism'. No more media mantras about 'unicorns', 'fundraisers', 'spectacular gains', etc. Contemporary societies – and this is even more true in a post-pandemic context – need social and community ties, whether their members are from Douala, Marseille, or Montréal. Entrepreneurial activism exists, first, as a way of answering these current issues, and then, second, as a way of supporting the entrepreneurial projects that individuals or groups attempt to undertake.

The term 'start-up' usually refers to an entrepreneurial project that has clearly defined growth ambitions, and one that is associated with a technology capable of bringing about a change of scale and creating an important need for capital to ensure development. In this book, however, the term 'start-up' has an acceptation that is independent of these characteristics. We use it with an eye to its etymology, focusing on the notion of start-up projects of any nature and in any sector of activity – that are launched and carried out through the determination of the persons who undertake them. The term 'community' brings with it what binds people together, what allows for a sense of belonging that is necessary to their identity and that fosters social interaction. Entrepreneurial activism reverses the usual way of thinking about the coupling of these two terms. The community comes first in the entrepreneurial project, the start-up comes later.

Thus *Community 1st Start-up 2nd* is a rallying cry for all those who want to participate in developing an alternative to the dominant model of business creation. It is addressed to future entrepreneurs as well as to those in charge of entrepreneurial support programmes who wish to foster a new spirit of business creation and a new way of setting in motion promising initiatives.

In a word, through this book we hope to make our own contribution to a movement in which we firmly believe.

Franck Barès, Bernard Cova and Anicet Nemani

1

UNDERSTANDING BRAND COMMUNITIES

The objective of this introductory chapter is to explain what brand communities are and to examine how they can be made to emerge, and also to distinguish the related phenomena of tribes, online communities, communities of practices and other types of fan groups. The first section of the chapter will be devoted to defining them conceptually. In the second section, it will then be possible to focus directly on brand communities in order to develop an understanding of how they function. The third section will introduce the central issue of this book: the methods for creating a community around a new brand.

A CONTEMPORARY HISTORY OF THE NOTION OF COMMUNITY

It is worth beginning by questioning the notion of community, for an overabundance of information and uses have made it somewhat of a cliché. Indeed, the term is used to refer to a variety of different and sometimes even contrary realities. During the last three decades, it has nevertheless shaped the perceptions and the models of analysts examining society and the market. Yet before the advent of this plurality of communities, other terms were used.

The Prehistory: Subcultures and Fandoms

Before the 1980s, the term 'subculture' was used in the rare texts addressing issues related to collective consumption phenomena. The term refers to groups of individuals on the margin of the dominant culture who share a separate style and a different set of values. The notion of a subculture makes it possible to qualify the specific culture of these subgroups inside society in general. These subgroups have a certain number of common cultural traits, but also more specific ones, which are not found in other social groups. Usually, these groups are viewed as deviant. During the 1970s, for example, British youth was the crucible for the punk and glam-rock subcultures, and for the powerful Rasta subculture imported to England by Caribbean migrants. Parallel to this, the phenomenon of fandom or fan clubs, which has been well documented by Henry Jenkins,[1] came to be understood as the subculture associated with a group of fans, that is, with everything connected to a specific group of people's favourite sphere of activity and to their way of organizing or creating it. Thus, the notion of a subculture was used in reference to clubs of soccer fans, opera fanatics, bikers and other groups with marginal behaviours. At the time, marketing revolved around segments of average consumers – with the well-known reference to housewives – and showed no interest in the minority phenomenon of subcultures.

Today the term 'subculture' is still used, but mostly in sociology. For instance, it is used to refer to geeks – fans of imaginary fantasy worlds who have a passion for new technologies. On the other hand, the term 'fandom' has a relatively wide diffusion in contemporary societies thanks to the universe of TV and movie series, with *Star Wars* standing as a prime example. Changes during the last 20 years have led certain commentators to insist on the central role of fanaticism. The phenomenon of fanaticism can be illustrated by the numerous events during which individuals go to extreme lengths to disguise themselves so that they can spend several hours or even days playing the part of characters such as Darth Vader, Spock or even Super Mario. Taken separately, each of these cases seems to depend on the extreme practices of a limited number of individuals with marginal behaviours. Yet the multiplication of these behaviours and their diffusion in every sector of contemporary society bring into question their abnormality and make fanaticism a commonplace phenomenon. There are no longer any average persons who can be contrasted with fans: we are all fans of something.

The Era of Tribes

At the end of the 1980s, the topic of tribes begins to generate discussion. It is important to recall that the period between the end of the 1980s and the beginning of the 1990s sees the peak of individualism in Western societies and that, in line with almost all sociological analyses, marketing is oriented towards an approach favouring personalized relationships with each consumer. There is a move from mass markets to masses of markets, each individual becoming a specific target that can be identified and documented. It is during this period that customer relationship management developed, a field that required businesses to invest significant amounts of money in information systems that centralize, stock and analyse huge volumes of data on existing clients and on prospective ones, that is, on everything from consumption activities to contact logs. Businesses must then make this data available in real time, which leads to the personalization of product and service offers as well as business procedures. At this point, the web is still at the 1.0 version stage, with Internet sites operating in read-only mode. There is no interaction between parties. The one creates, and the other reads; the one offers, and the other buys. The only harbinger of the 2.0 revolution to come seems to be the discussion forums.

In this context of a frenzied individualism reinforced by technological developments, it may appear contradictory to refer to community. Yet some studies in everyday life sociology point to the advent of the era of tribes. Thus, at a time when every commentator on 1990s society is highlighting the incredible rise of individualism, Michel Maffesoli[2] detects numerous signs of a contrary tendency that he calls 'tribalism'. According to Maffesoli, far from being satisfied with an isolated individual life, contemporary human beings are creating a profusion of opportunities to share experiences together and to live these experiences in a highly emotional mode. In choosing to use the term 'tribes' to describe these more or less ephemeral gatherings, Maffesoli adopts an anthropological perspective on this phenomenon. Today's tribes are groups in which individuals interact with each other, develop strong emotional bonds and have shared passions and similar experiences. However, in contrast to the sense of belonging characteristic of traditional tribes, which is unique and impossible to dissolve, today's tribalism sees individuals jump from one tribe to another. In this new sense, a tribe is a group of individuals who are heterogenous in terms of their sociodemographic characteristics but interconnected through a common emotion. And such a tribe is capable of collective action. Therefore, it is the opposite of a social class or market segment that only brings together homogenous individuals.

In the United States and France, studies on consumption and marketing begin to integrate the notion of tribalism in the middle of the 1990s. At the time, tribalism appears to be at best marginal, at worst highly questionable. Consumer tribes can be identified in society and through consumption practices – there are Goths, Mac fans, Jeep drivers, etc. – but few businesses adopt marketing approaches that can be described as tribal. Some emblematic cases make it possible to put forward the idea that consumers united around the same passion can provide a way to develop and sustain a marketing approach: Harley Davidson and the HOG (Harley Owners' Group), the Wizards of the Coast and their game *Magic: The Gathering*, etc.

The Invention of Online Communities

With the advent of Web 2.0 at the end of the 1990s, there is a shift from the static web to the social web. A dimension of sharing and information exchange enters the Internet, with newly formed or reconsolidated groups emerging thanks to virtual exchanges on forums and to mailing lists, and then by way of blogs and other platforms. From the perspective of the evangelists for the new information and communications technologies, people like Howard Rheingold,[3] these virtual groups are similar to communities – they are in fact 'virtual communities'. However, if one adheres to the tradition in sociology, the notion of community refers to a collective that is founded on geographical and emotional proximity and that involves direct, concrete, authentic interaction between its members. Therefore, associating the term 'community' with the virtual or with being online appears contradictory. But Rheingold sees the notion of a virtual community as legitimate because if the idea of a community accessible only via his computer screen sounded cold to him at first, he learned quickly that people can feel passionately about e-mail and Internet conferences. They care about the people they met through their computer. Thus, in Rheingold's view, the emotion in these online exchanges justifies the use of the term 'community'.

From this point onward, debate focuses on the question whether these online groups are simulated communities or imagined communities. The main objection to the use of the term 'community' revolves around the fact that individuals online are not necessarily aware that they form a community or that they belong to one. This does not prevent the diffusion and the ever-increasing use of the expression 'virtual community'. It is used to define groups of people who communicate by way of emails, online forums or telephone conversations for professional, social, educational or other reasons. Today the term 'online community', which is now preferred to 'virtual community', is used to refer to a wide variety of groups brought together by shared lifestyles and connected consumption interests and in which discursive practices involve negotiation. Thus, there has been movement away from the idea that shared emotions are central to the existence of online communities.

By the end of the 1990s, Internet communitarianism had started to attract attention, particularly among marketers and managers. It is clear that virtual communities have numerous advantages and that there were interesting possibilities in digital acquisition and consumer retention. Over time, virtual communities gradually become essential to communications strategies. They are especially important to the extent that they make it possible for consumers to exchange and create content for themselves.

While the contemporary reference to tribes brings back into use an anthropological notion, the reference to virtual communities has a connection to nineteenth-century sociology. In both cases, the terms used today are partially freed of their original meanings so that they can be added to the manager's toolkit. It is the sharing of emotions and the mixture of profiles that justify the current use of the terms 'community' and 'tribe'.

The Advent of Communities of Practices

The term 'community' becomes more and more prevalent – and not only in the discourse of the specialists dedicated to the new information and communications technologies. A return and a parallel reinterpretation of the notion of community take place in the area of knowledge management at and between businesses. As of the 1990s, businesses begin to see that the communities of practice highlighted in the work of Etienne Wenger[4] provide one of the most effective means of sharing knowledge and best practices. These communities are groups of individuals who share a common interest in a practice or sector of activity: the use of a product or brand, process improvement, commercial performance, new service development, product enhancement, supplier qualification, etc. As a result, professionals begin to debate the merits of their practices. They reflect on what they are doing, propose improvements, discuss problems and help each other out. They exchange with each other about their experiences in order to find ways to solve difficulties. These exchanges all take place in a non-hierarchical context of discussion between peers who come from different divisions of the business. A community of practice functions transversally with business systems, which means that it facilitates exchanges and allows people to communicate freely.

According to Etienne Wenger, communities of practice come in a wide variety of different forms. There are communities of practice that have very little structure. People get together on Fridays after work for a beer and talk. They don't say we're a community of practice, they say we talk. But if you listen to what's going on, then there's a lot of discussion, a lot of problems to be solved and a lot of improvement to be made to the practice. It's very unstructured and in some cases it works very well. At the other end of the spectrum, there are communities that are facilitated by professional facilitators. There is an agenda, a list of issues to discuss. It's very structured. There is often a manager who acts as a sponsor and connects the community directly to the company's hierarchy. Then why not use the term 'club' to refer to this type of group? Once again, it may be a question of highlighting the presence of shared emotion. Without it, these gatherings of professionals would be no more than meetings, for it is emotion that unites participants together to form a community centred on shared practices. Moreover, the mix of formal memberships, of business divisions and functions, often makes it possible to circumvent power relations.

The Rising Power of Brand Communities

Renewed and reinvigorated by the new information and communications technologies, the phenomenon of community continues to gain ground outside of the virtual world. Indeed, at the beginning of the twenty-first century, a new concept revolutionizes the way of *doing* marketing: the brand community. Defined as groups of individuals who share the same passion for a brand and who create a parallel social universe with its own values, rituals, hierarchies and even its own vocabulary, brand communities break free of any geographical limits thanks to the Internet. Thus, a brand community such as AFOL – Adult Fans of Lego – can bring together millions of people from all across the world.

Contrary to the researchers who originated the notion of virtual communities, the ones who first conceptualized the phenomenon of brand communities tried to maintain continuity with the tradition in sociology.[5] For these other researchers, a group of consumers who unite around a brand can only be considered a brand community if the following conditions are met: 1) its members have an awareness that they form a separate group; 2) there is a moral obligation for members to help each other and 3) the group has rituals and traditions. The Jeep community provides a clear-cut example. Its members identify themselves as Jeepers and are prepared to help each other when necessary. They organize large rallies (Jeep Jamborees) every year, and they greet other Jeepers with a special salute (the Jeep Wave) when they meet them. This characterization makes it possible to distinguish brands that have an authentic community from brands for which there is an aggregate of individuals who discuss together on a website or a digital platform, but without having any shared emotions.

Brand communities became an established social phenomenon. In August 2004, their relevance to firms was validated by the annual *Business Week* ranking of the world's top brands.[6] The magazine maintained that:

> [C]onsumers are changing how they view and even relate to brands. They remain purchasers of products, true, but through the power of the Internet and as a result of cultural and demographic shifts, many consumers now actively form larger communities around their favorite brands.

Further research demonstrated the connection between belonging to a community and having brand loyalty. The existence of a brand community became a major criterion for measuring the strength of brands and was recognized as having a significant impact on their financial value.

Although brand communities constitute a new type of community that promotes the social life of brands, it is necessary to avoid an error frequently made by market and social observers, the one that consists in characterizing as a brand community any group of people exchanging information or discussing issues related to a brand. The development of the Internet and of social media such as Facebook and Twitter has significantly increased the possibilities for people to communicate about or around brands, and there is a tendency to reproduce the blogger–follower model. However, this type of communication produces a form of sociability that it would be inappropriate to describe as communitarian. Some researchers use the term 'consociality' to characterize social relations in what are incorrectly called 'online' or 'virtual communities' and to distinguish these groups from brand communities. Other researchers have proposed the notion of a brand public[7] to depict the online aggregation of a large number of isolated people that have a common focus – a brand – but do not necessarily interact.

Support for Communities: Social Networks

The unfettered extension of the notion of community, particularly in discussions of brand communities, led the advocates of digital marketing to reappropriate it. This new perspective pays no heed to the sociological roots of the term 'community'. Instead, a community is understood as the equivalent of a digital social network that gives individuals the possibility to connect, discuss and engage in relations with other Internet users. At businesses, people begin to speak of 'developing virtual communities' or 'social networks'. For some, a community is nothing more than a set of *Likes* attributed to a contest on a Facebook page. The phenomenon of influencers, whose style allows them to create and band together communities of fans who appreciate their personality and their often trenchant opinions, causes more trouble for marketers, who would like to benefit from their aura. Social networks need to have their own idols. They have produced a new generation of stars and influencers who're often called 'YouTubers' in reference to the record audiences they generate on YouTube. Thus digital marketing seeks to tap into such communities by co-opting these opinion leaders.

Yet although communities and social networks can be compatible with each other in a marketing strategy, they are not the same thing. Indeed, individuals group together as enthusiasts of a film, a brand or a sports team, or simply by having the same main interests, but no social network alone can monopolize all the possibilities for exchanges between community members. In the digital world, each platform, each social media site, has its own language, one that helps community members express their passion and interest. The difference can be illustrated by the case of a community of croissant fans in Quebec, Canada – yes, such a community exists! To a certain extent, the various social networks can amplify and extend this passion for croissants, but it is essential to note that each network is used to communicate about a specific aspect of this passion. Thus, on Twitter, the community members can announce in real time that they are presently eating a croissant. On Facebook, they can show which types of croissants they like the most. On Foursquare or on another geolocation platform, they can show where they currently enjoy a croissant. On Instagram, they can post photos of themselves with croissants. On YouTube, they can download a video explaining how to eat a croissant. On LinkedIn, they can include knowing how to eat croissants in their list of competencies. Certain businesses have clearly understood this form of social network specialization. For example, Adidas interacts with its brand community through a variety of networks, using each one in a specific way.[8] It uses its TikTok account to target young fashion and streetwear fans – 75% of TikTok users being under 25 years old. It mobilizes Facebook and Instagram to reach other audiences with other themes.

Each platform and each social media network can contribute something to the life of a community, but in itself, it does not constitute the community, being no more than a specific expression of it. This means that it is important to distinguish between the work performed by a community manager and that performed by a social media manager, two roles that are often confused with each other. A community manager is the ambassador for brand discourse, the person at the business who is responsible for the online and offline life of the brand community. This person's activities revolve around facilitating exchanges between community members on different social networks and increasing the size of the community. As for a social media manager, he or she is the person who searches through and analyses what is said on selected social media, the person who is responsible for the strategy used to increase the visibility of the business on these social networks and for orienting them towards greater engagement with the brand through communitarian action and other types of undertaking. Thus a social media manager's range of actions is much wider and more business oriented.

We hope that this historical overview of the use of the term 'community' in contemporary society gives readers a better understanding of the notion of a brand community.

BRAND COMMUNITIES

The acceleration of change in every area – technology, institutions, geopolitics – constantly disrupts and reconfigures the human world, producing an identity crisis for numerous individuals. One major aspect of this decomposition concerns work, which has lost its stability and become what Zygmunt Bauman[9] has aptly called 'liquid' – it has no solidity and seems to slip through people's fingers. Indeed, life-time jobs at the same firm have long disappeared, and the role of work in human identity has progressively diminished as jobs become increasingly meaningless. As David Graeber[10] shows, many workers are spending their lives doing useless tasks with no real interest or meaning, all the while fully aware of the superficiality of their contribution to society.

As a result, individuals turn to a new source of identity – consumption – the objective of which is not the satisfaction of the kind of needs for which people went to the supermarket during the 1950s, but instead the fulfilment of an identity role related to leisure, culture, sports, etc. Individuals attempt to satisfy all the ordinary passions that require them to purchase equipment, tickets for events, subscriptions, etc. They pursue what they consider to be meaningful experiences. Thus we have gone from a society in which the main basis of identity is work to one in which it is consumption. But consumption is articulated around a strange source of attraction – brands – whose role as resources in the identity construction of individuals has become major. Certain brands give meaning to lived experiences and to life in general; they are cultural referents in contemporary society. It is in this sense that they have taken the place of certain institutions that are no longer capable of helping to make our lives and our world intelligible. Some are more respected than governmental institutions and have an important influence on daily life.

Therefore, brand communities are much more than marketing tools. Indeed, they are social units in which, whether it be online or offline, individuals can share, be acknowledged and feel a sense of belonging to a group. Of course, the members of these communities come together around a 'commercial' totem; however, this commercial dimension is far from being the most important one for them. Brand communities allow their members to reestablish a level of stability in their lives in a context in which everything is moving fast. This is why their members spend a great deal of time and effort participating in community activities.

Brand community activities mobilize the competencies and the individual and collective forms of expertise possessed by community members. Four large categories of brand community activities have been identified[11]:

- Social networking: welcoming (admitting new members and accompanying them in their integration into the community), support (providing emotional or functional support to community members) and politeness (moderating and orienting the behaviour of members to ensure that they respect the community's spirit and its norms);

- Impression management: evangelization (converting and inspiring new persons) and justification (providing members with reasons to justify the sacrifice of time and money for the tribal passion);

- Community management: attribution of roles (marking differences in terms of roles and competencies), milestones (creating founding events and ones that serve as markers for the experience of each member), symbolization (highlighting symbols and rituals that facilitate integration into the community), and narration (creating and sharing the community's stories and its history);

- Use of the product: maintenance (sharing recipes and other devices that make it possible to use and maintain products), personalization (introducing modifications that make it possible to personalize products) and commercialization (creating an internal market for used products and new services).

Contrary to the marketer's dream of having a tribal chief or a head of a community who can be transformed into an opinion leader in accordance with the influencer model, most brand communities operate in a way that distributes a multiplicity of roles among different members, an approach that makes every member into a potential influencer. For example, in every community there are members with the role of storytellers who relate the group's narratives. There are also members who play the role of historians who preserve the community's memory and codify its rites and rituals. Many different roles exist for community members. Commensurate with his or her status in the group, each member has the power to influence the rest of the community.

Brand communities are in no way homogenous. Inside these communities, various subgroups develop, with different levels of involvement and different roles. Companies such as Harley-Davidson have brand communities that are organized in concentric circles. At the centre, there are the hardcore members, the consumers who are the most involved, the fanatics who 'live, sleep, and make love' with the brand and who consider themselves the 'guardians of the temple'. Just outside the centre, there is a small circle of consumers with a heavy involvement with the brand, ones who are passionately committed to it and who play the role of brand missionaries, in particular by hosting chats and blogs. The third circle is larger and mostly composed of consumers who occasionally participate in community events, but who nevertheless see themselves as 'true members'. Finally, there is a loose and more or less invisible conglomeration of atomized consumers who experience their membership in the community in an imaginary way, for example, by touching their H.O.G. (Harley Owners' Group) card. Other businesses function instead with clans that belong to the same community, but that signal their different tastes and styles in online and offline manifestations of their opposition to others that tend to be hectic and highly visible.

Thus brand communities are far from uniform. In fact, they are a crucible of tensions and conflicts:

● Loyalty in opposition to another brand (that which best defines a brand community is its opposition to another brand and its community);

● The legitimacy or illegitimacy of being a brand consumer, which can lead to the rejection of a part of the population ('true believer' or 'non-believer'?);

- The desire to be marginal (the determined effort of a small, anti-conformist circle to avoid being reappropriated);

- Brand politization (where a brand community has a marked political orientation);

- The abandoned community (the brand community that continues to exist even though the brand, for example, the Chrysler PT Cruiser, has disappeared from the company portfolio);

- The counterpower of the brand community.

With respect to the last point, it is clear that 'brand ownership' is one of the most important issues connected to the rise of these communities. Indeed, brand communities demand to have control of brands. They have increasing power over distribution and more and more of the competencies that used to be the preserve of marketers. The collective feeling of brand ownership, at the expense of the business, can be the source of numerous conflicts.

The case of *La Scala* in Milan offers a significant example of the negative impact of such a situation. At *La Scala*, *loggionisti* – audience members seated in the upper gallery (the *loggione*) – have always been known as merciless judges who are prone to express their displeasure. Formidable opera connoisseurs, *loggionisti* do not hesitate to voice their disapproval by booing artists. During the last decade, there has been such an increase in virulent gestures of contestation addressed to opera singers that, frightened by this vindictive audience, these artists no longer want to perform at *La Scala*. Recently, the new general manager of *La Scala* stated that because of the *loggionisti*, five out of twelve of the world's best opera singers no longer want to practice their art at the iconic opera house. And yet it is a love for *La Scala* that motivates the repeated contestations. For these opera fans – for these consumers – it is not acceptable that a brand so important for society and for themselves should be subject to transformations that alter its very essence. Seeing themselves as the owners of the brand, they feel free to use relatively violent means to protect it, even if this is to the detriment of the legal owners of the brand, the company to which it belongs, and the executives who manage it – not to mention other consumers of the brand whom they consider illegitimate. Indeed, in their view the choices made by management, which are oriented towards less traditional and more international shows, divert *La Scala* from its main mission, preserving *bel canto*.

However, it is essential not to view brand communities uniquely from the perspective of for-profit organizations, even if these organizations are cultural. The Internet has created innumerable possibilities for people to form groups, and this has led to the development of alternative forms of consumption that are based on sharing. The main goal of these sharing communities – ones like Bookcrossing, Couchsurfing and Geocaching – is to have an impact on society, but their efforts have a rebound effect on the market, which is often disturbed by offers that are free or have no commercial purpose. These projects are generated by communities of consumers who meet on the Internet to devise credible alternatives to offers made by businesses. Some sharing communities succeed in acquiring such a level of world renown that they become veritable brands – community brands – that are in direct competition with commercial ones. This is not only the case for brands from the open-source world, ones such as Linux and Firefox that compete with Microsoft, it is also the case for project brands. For example, to the detriment of the professionals in the sector, Couchsurfing has upset the accommodations offer throughout the world. In place of for-profit consumption that benefits businesses, these brands substitute a form of consumption that is based on sharing between individuals.

CONSTRUCTING A COMMUNITY AROUND A BRAND

The phenomenon of brand communities makes managers and marketers dream, but numerous errors result from a lack of understanding of the mechanisms underlying this type of community. One of the main errors consists in using traditional management and marketing methods to understand a phenomenon whose reality lies well outside the market in a context that is more societal than commercial. The main factors leading to a successful analysis are linked to a valid understanding of the elements that are there at the beginning. Is there an already existing community united around the brand? If not, is it possible to detect communitarian dimensions in the areas of activity connected to the brand offer? This analysis is even more crucial if it is a question of a brand in the launching phase. Three main types of communitarian strategy can then be distinguished:

1. the strategy of capitalizing on the existing community, if by luck there is one;

2. the strategy of co-opting a community of individuals who are passionate about an activity and

3. the strategy of creating a community.

Capitalizing on an Existing Community United Around the Brand

To capitalize on an existing community that is united around the brand, it is first necessary to avoid adopting a generalizing view that construes the community as a homogenous group. This makes it possible to identify the different subgroups and the often conflictual dynamics that are present in a community. It is also necessary to avoid falling prey to the opinion leader myth, the belief that it suffices to target one person for the role of 'managing' the community. Next, a complete reversal of the usual way of thinking is required: the main capital of a brand is not founded on products and services, but instead on the bonds that have been created between the members of the brand community. It is this linking value that attracts consumers. As demonstrated by Ducati (see Box 1), a company that opted for this strategy at the beginning of the twenty-first century, it is essential to place the community at the very heart of the action plan in order to make it grow. Thus it is of paramount importance to increase the number of opportunities for members to interact, both online and offline. It is also advisable to adopt an approach based on the management of rituals at various levels of community structuring (at the local, national and international levels, through centres of interest, etc.). As time goes by, it is essential to avert the risk of the community withdrawing into itself, a situation that can lead to a marketing impasse where actors are not replaced. Harley-Davidson is currently exposed to such a risk because consumer-bikers enamoured of the myth of freedom seem to give little reason to younger generations to want to interact with them.

Box 1. Capitalizing on the Ducati Brand Community.

'We're not talking about customers, but about fans. And in marketing terms, who is the typical Ducati fan? At first, I wanted to do customer segmentation, but it wasn't possible. The range of profiles goes from the rich customer who shows off his Ducati during a vacation to the simple worker who saves up little by little to buy the motorcycle of his dreams. Which is why I prefer to speak of the Ducati tribe. By a tribe I mean a group of persons that have something in common. At the centre of the tribe, there is the totem, the Ducati. That said, the product is not what defines the tribe, it is the identity link between the different members of this tribe'.[12] These are the words of Federico Minoli, who was the CEO of Ducati at the beginning of the twenty-first century. Created almost a century ago, Ducati was almost bankrupt at the end of the 1990s when Minoli took charge of it for TPG, an American investment firm. Since then, Ducati has found the road back to success and become a giant in its market.

Thus Minoli put all his bets on the brand community, which he preferred to call a 'tribe', immediately appointing, not a marketing manager, but a tribe director. Indeed, without the possibility of using communications strategies targeting the general public, an approach that would have been too expensive, Ducati relied on the hype generated by its web-site (www.ducati.com) to relaunch the business and also on a set of events, including the *Ducati Weekends*, that allowed it to build a huge online community around a very active offline community. According to Minoli, 'It's the members of the tribe that do the work. That's what's amazing. Let me give you an example: recently, there was a big report about us on the front page of the weekend edition of the *Daily Telegraph*. It was about the participation of a Ducati bike in a rally for old motorcycles. In public relations terms, it was something terrific for us. Even more so given that we have neither the money nor the media weight necessary to determine where this type of story is placed in a newspaper. But our article appeared on the front page because the journalist belonged to the Ducati tribe'.[13] In 2010, the fervent supporters of Ducati form more than a thousand clubs in the world, whereas there were only 40 of them 20 years ago. These clubs are very different from one another, going from ones like the 'Neo-fascists of Rome' to ones like the 'San Francisco Gays'. They have the right to create their own tee-shirts depicting the brand, and the Internet allows clubs to communicate with one another and even meet in the real world. For example, a club in Rome was able to bring numerous Italians to a rally organized in Daytona, Florida.

Moreover, for Minoli, the community had to be used for more than just communications. It also had to be mobilized to help define the authentic Ducati. This made it possible to identify the essential features that make a motorcycle a true Ducati: the L alignment of the motor's cylinders, the steel-tube frame, the (patented!) sound of the motor and the exclusive Ducati DESMO (desmodromic) valve system. These distinctive features also belong to the competition models that are the crowning glory of the moto GP bike brand.

Next, Minoli expanded the offer to include any type of product – and in particular clothing – that allows customers to participate in Ducati rituals. Thus Ducati makes more than just motorcycles; it also makes a whole range of special accessories and articles of clothing for racing (the *linea Ducati Corsa*). For these products, the company did a great deal of photo work to make an inventory of its passionate enthusiasts' fashion choices and transform these choices into a line of clothing and accessories. These products are sold exclusively by Ducati stores, the largest of which is located in

Indonesia – proof that the brand has a global impact. Finally, passionate enthusiasts can visit the factory near Bologna, where everything is there to see except the Ducati Competition section, whose operations are kept secret. Through a small window, visitors can get no more than a glimpse of what goes on there. The factory has been transformed into a veritable place of worship for the community.

Passionate Ducati enthusiasts benefit from very close contact with company staff who are also members of the community. For Moto GP competitions and particularly for the one in Italy that takes place on the Mugello Circuit located between Bologna and Florence, Ducati reserves 4,000 places for these enthusiasts, with 600 going to its employees who, among other things, are in charge of choreographed stadium events to support the brand's drivers. Stopping in front of the fans in the grandstands, drivers do burnouts by accelerating rapidly with the wheels of their now stationary bikes spinning in place, a stunt that leaves a lot of burnt rubber on the track. The tribal leaders are usually people who work for Ducati. Thus all the company's engineers are passionate enthusiasts (see Table 1).

Table 1. The Ducati Model of Tribal Marketing.

The Conventional Model	The Tribal Model
Recruit	Co-opt
Employee/worker	Member of the tribe
Client/customer	Member of the tribe
Client–business relationship	Member–member relationship
Communicating with clients/customers	Sharing emotions
Marketing activities	Rituals
Factory/museum	Place of worship/pilgrimage
Keeping fans at a distance	Integrating members
Sport	Passion
Manager	Shaman

Source: Cova and Shankar (2020).[4]

Co-opting an Existing Community With No Initial Link to the Brand

To co-opt a community that already exists but that has no link to the brand, it is necessary to begin by locating potentially interesting communities with members who might consider the brand a means to improve their ability to share their passion. This is what Nike did when it undertook to find communities united around a passion for soccer. After attempting to create a community around the *Joga Bonito* (Beautiful Game) during the 2006 World Cup in Germany, Nike evaluated the potential of different groups of fans. It chose to work with those fans who support the Corinthians club in Brazil, who are over 30 million strong. To help these fans celebrate the 100th anniversary of the club in 2010, Nike created the *Republic Popular do Corinthians*. The brand introduced an imaginary constitution for the fictional republic, a passport for each member, as well as a currency, and it even nominated a president – who happened to be the actual president of Brazil at the time, Lula. The benefits were extremely interesting for Nike, which saw this initiative as an effective way to develop its brand community.

Businesses that want to co-opt a community for the benefit of their brand do not need to go overboard by following Nike's example. However, it is advisable for them to proceed in three phases:

1. an ethnographic phase to develop an understanding of the targeted community's codes and begin the process of gaining acceptance;

2. a co-design phase in which certain community members are invited to help prepare the offer of brand events and products for the community; and

3. a development phase in which instead of launching communications campaigns, community support for all types of action is developed.

The Quebec restaurant chain *La Cage* did something similar with fans of the Montreal Canadiens hockey team. The Canadiens are almost a religion for people who live in Montreal or elsewhere in the Province of Quebec. Indeed, hockey is an essential part of life in Quebec and the coach of the Canadiens is quoted in the media just as often as the premier of the province. Since 1995, when Quebec City lost its hockey team, the importance of the Montreal Canadiens, now the only Quebec team in the National Hockey League, has increased even more. Thus, *La Cage* decided to co-opt Canadiens fans by offering them eight free chicken wings whenever the team scores five goals or more during a regular season or a play-off game.[15] At first sight, this strategy may appear anecdotal. Yet everyone in Montreal knows the Canadiens and shares, at least to some degree, in the city's hockey mania, bringing *La Cage* a community base of more than 1.5 million members. The brand could have never hoped for such an impact without this co-option strategy.

Creating a Community Around a New Brand

Capitalizing on an existing brand community or co-opting an existing community with no initial link to the brand may seem to be effective approaches for businesses, but attempting to create a brand community from scratch rarely leads to success. Yet businesses that adopt this strategy spend a lot of money, particularly on proprietary platforms. Every day they develop thousands of new groups and original pages on social media, but these efforts remain largely ineffective because, unless games and other contests are added to the mix, consumers do not feel a need to join. Communities must be created 'with' – not 'for' – consumers.

Constructing a relevant community requires patience because before focusing on desired outcomes, it is necessary to begin by working in society outside the market. This runs completely contrary to the approach adopted by most businesses. Indeed, instead of considering the market for launching a startup, the entrepreneur must first take action at the social level to create a movement. Throughout this book, we attempt to detail and analyse this approach.

We can begin by an example that is obviously imperfect, but that has the advantage of making it possible to specify the idea underlying this approach. Created by Will Dean[16] in 2011, the brand

Tough Mudder is an obstacle course approximately 15 kilometres long that is inspired by the one used to train the United Kingdom Special Forces. According to Dean, with a total of 25 obstacles it is the most difficult endurance event in the world. The obstacle course is not only a severe test of participants' physical endurance, but also an extremely difficult challenge to their mental capacities and their resistance to pain. During the 3-hour event, participants must dive into a giant ice bath, climb four-metre-high walls, cross a waterway using a rope suspended in the air, crawl through tunnels filled with mud or water, carry tree trunks and even avoid electric shocks of up to 10,000 volts! To register for the event, participants must pay €150. And it works! Tough Mudder now has 6 million participants. Called 'Mudders', they come from all around the world. Among them, one finds seasoned athletes, but most of the participants are executives and office workers who spend long days sitting in front of their computer screens in air-conditioned buildings. Moreover, although some financial excesses recently incited Will Dean to sell his business, the example of Tough Mudder makes it possible to highlight five major operations that are necessary for success if one undertakes the difficult task of creating a new brand community.

1. Advocate a Cause and Launch a Movement

To cultivate a community, the first step is to choose the right area of activity. There are some types of activities, in particular ones related to the sale of basic commodities, for which the idea of community is ineffectual or even absurd. But there are others for which activity communities already exist. Will Dean highlighted this point when he insisted on the necessity of using a 'tribe' to launch a movement. Before Tough Mudder was launched, there were already more than a million persons participating in obstacle courses in the United States, events combining cross-country racing with endurance tests from military training. Thus, when the business and its brand were still only in their embryonic phase, there already existed a community. It was a question of approaching the community and gaining its acceptance so that the creation of the start-up had legitimacy, which meant that this had to be undertaken by someone belonging to the community. Will Dean understood this because he was a passionate enthusiast of obstacle courses long before he founded Tough Mudder.

The same dynamism allowed Will Dean to capture the underlying issue that motivated this community: the problem of how to help individuals overcome the physical lethargy caused by managerial work. A graduate of the famous Harvard Business School, Dean was able to have numerous discussions with top students from previous years who had become 'professional zombies', in the sense that their office work, mostly performed while they were seated in front of a computer screen, was boring them to death. Finding a way for these knowledge workers to rediscover their bodies is the issue that Will Dean committed himself to addressing, a cause that brought together thousands of Mudders.

2. Recruit Volunteers and Ask for Their Collaboration

To cultivate a community, the second step is to accelerate the consolidation of the group through collaboration. The more that consumers collaborate, whether it be with one another or with those carrying out the project, the stronger their sense of community. Every Tough Mudder event takes place in a natural setting far from cities and requires extensive logistical support for tasks such as the following: registering participants, distributing competition bibs, managing the movement of competitors to the starting line, supplying water to them, giving them encouragement as they attempt to get beyond obstacles, handing out headbands after each successfully completed stage in the event, and providing beer and food at the end. Consumers work as volunteers when they perform these activities that are essential to the smooth running of the event.

Will Dean takes every opportunity he can to thank the MVPs (Most Valuable Players) for their collaboration. Moreover, he openly states in a YouTube motivation video that Tough Mudder would be impossible without volunteers. His insistence on the importance of their role gives the consumer-volunteers a strong sense that they are an integral part of the brand project. And making it possible to experience collaboration with the brand and with other consumers over the course of an event day is also a means to develop the linking value of the brand.

3. Foster Online and Offline Interactions

To cultivate a community, the third step is to give the innumerable groups who have participated in an event like an obstacle course the opportunity to connect with one another and form an authentic community. Studies have shown that the more members interact with one another, the more they become active and remain loyal to the brand.

For a sense of belonging to a distinct group to develop, it is necessary for the community to have a simple name that brings to mind the brand or corporate name. Thus consumers united around Tough Mudder are called Mudders, and as a community, they are referred to as the Mudder Nation. Mudders flood Facebook pages with accounts of what they have endured during Tough Mudder events and with comments on specific obstacles. The firm concentrates its efforts mostly on YouTube, showing videos filmed by its adepts. Moreover, it also gives Mudders the means to interact online, mobilizing more than ten photographers for each event to provide each Mudder with at least a dozen photos of his or her feats of endurance. These photos are optimized for use on Facebook and Instagram.

The interactions are not limited to event days, for they also take place during participants' preparation for Tough Mudder events. Offline, there are gyms dedicated to Tough Mudder where people can do specific exercises to prepare themselves for these events, and online, there is the video series *Coachified*.

4. Develop Rituals

To cultivate a community, the fourth step is the development of rituals. Ever since sociology first became a field of research, rituals have been recognized as necessary for developing and maintaining social relations. It has also been acknowledged that all social groups need rituals to affirm and reaffirm their existence and to reinforce their members' sense of belonging. Belief, the reduction of uncertainty and facilitating social integration are the three functions of what have been traditionally described as religious rites or rituals. However, there are many researchers today who maintain that secular rituals also have these three dimensions.

Will Dean has introduced multiple offline and online rites. Offline, he has all the participants in Tough Mudder obstacle courses recite together the Mudder pledge before beginning to compete. After competitors cross the finish line, a volunteer places a Tough Mudder headband on them. Online every Monday, competitors can post photos of themselves wearing the Tough Mudder headbands they have won. This photo-sharing opportunity is called *Headband Monday*. With more than 10,000 Mudders reported to be 'inked', another online ritual involves posting photos of Tough Mudder tattoos. Finally, after each Tough Mudder event – sometimes even weeks later – competitors engage in a ritual exchange of photos showing their injuries.

5. Insert Linking Value into the Value Proposition and Put it at the Heart of the Business Model

To cultivate a community, the fifth step is to sow the 'tribal seed' at the very beginning of the conception phase of the business project and its innovative offer. To do this, it is necessary to ensure that the linking value of the project is at the heart of the offer. Linking value refers to what the offer is worth in terms of constructing or reinforcing connections, even short-lived ones, between consumers. Some businesses are able to present offers with significant linking value, ones that create relationships between individuals who form the basis for a communitarian approach. It is a question of creating an offer, not for the much-vaunted isolated consumer who is the king of traditional marketing, but for groups of consumers who will share the experience offered by the business. This is what Tough Mudder does when it compels its adepts to participate in events as members of a team who must help each other confront obstacles.

Even though the registration fees are individualized, if a person wants to participate in a Tough Mudder obstacle course, he or she must register with a team. If the person has no teammate, he or she must create an online team or else, the day before the competition, go to a hotel chosen by the organization to find teammates for the competition. In the case of Tough Mudder, linking value is very important and highly visible. Moreover, it involves much more than a verbal or cognitive link because it is above all a physical one. Competitors who help one another get through obstacles in the mud share a corporal experience of community, something that remains registered in body memory for a long time.

In this chapter, we have sought to explain what brand communities are and how they function, and we have attempted to identify the steps that must be followed to allow them to emerge. As a first step, it is advisable to launch a business project as a movement to defend a cause. As a second step, project founders must call on consumers who are willing to help them with their business project. The third step requires envisaging numerous possibilities for interactions between consumers who have been mobilized for the project. In the fourth step, it is necessary to develop rituals that bring life to the community and allow it to be cultivated. Finally, in the fifth step, the conventional view of the isolated consumer must be rejected and the offer instead conceived as depending on consumers who have come together as a group, an approach that revolves around the intrinsic creation of linking value. Project founders do not have to follow these steps in the order they have been presented here. However, they must keep these steps constantly in mind and always think in terms of community before focusing on business creation.

NOTES

1. Henry Jenkins, *Textual Poachers: Television Fans & Participatory Culture*, London: Routledge, 1992.

2. Michel Maffesoli. *The Time of the Tribes: The Decline of Individualism in Mass Society*, London: Sage, 1995.

3. Howard Rheingold, *The Virtual Community: Homesteading on the Electronic Frontier*, Revised edition, Cambridge, MA: The MIT Press, 2000.

4. Etienne Wenger, *Communities of Practice: Learning, Meaning, and Identity*, Cambridge: Cambridge University Press, 1999.

5. Albert M. Muniz & Thomas C. O'Guinn, "Brand community." *Journal of Consumer Research* 27(4), 412–432, 2001.

6. *Business Week*, The Best Global Brands: Our Annual Ranking of the Top 100, 9–16 August 2004.

7. Adam Arvidsson & Alessandro Caliandro, "Brand public." *Journal of Consumer Research* 42(5), 727–748, 2016.

8. https://culture-rp.com/marketing-com/marketing-tribal-qui-se-ressemble-se-rassemble/

9. Zygmunt Bauman, *Liquid Modernity*, Chichester: John Wiley & Sons, 2013.

10. David Graeber, *Bullshit Jobs: A Theory*, London: Allen Lane, 2018.

11. Hope Jensen Schau, Albert M. Muñiz & Eric J. Arnould, "How brand community practices create value." *Journal of Marketing* 73(5), 30–51, 2009.

12. Bernard Cova, *Il Marketing Tribale*, 2nd edition, Milan: Gruppo 24 Ore, 2010.

13. Bernard Cova, *Il Marketing Tribale*, 2nd edition, Milan: Gruppo 24 Ore, 2010.

14. Bernard Cova & Avi Shankar, "Tribal marketing." In *Marketing Management: A Cultural Perspective*, 2nd edition, Lisa Penaloza, Nil Toulouse, & Luca M. Visconti (eds.), London: Routledge, pp. 168–182, 2020.

15. https://www.cage.ca/5-buts-8-ailes

16. Will Dean, *It Takes a Tribe: Building the Tough Mudder Movement*, New York, NY: Penguin, 2017.

2

DEFENDING A CAUSE AND
LAUNCHING A MOVEMENT

The traditional view is that communities are developed and maintained through primary social links with other persons – family members, friends, neighbours – and through direct interaction between these persons. With secondary sociality, notably on the job market, it is essentially indirect interaction that occurs, for persons interact in ways that are mediated by an activity, an office, a machine or a product. Usually, this second type of interaction generates imagined communities rather than real ones. In the context under discussion, an imagined community or a feeling of community is one that links individuals who consume the same product without ever interacting with one another. This is why the best way to construct a community around a start-up brand is to begin by taking action at the level of primary sociality. The idea is to have an impact on the direct interaction between persons well before engaging in any action on the market.

But how should a start-up brand go about doing this? Associations offer some of the best opportunities to succeed on this front. They constitute what sociologists[1] call a primary public space that is based on acquaintanceship. Entering an association means, first of all, taking the time and making the commitment to interact with others. As collectives, associations give individuals the opportunity to be close to one another and unite their efforts to accomplish something new or protect something that already exists. Today associations are often groups that combine elements from micro-social movements that are not great utopic movements like the ones founded on class interests in the nineteenth century, but instead small local ones whose aim is direct, immediate action that is not explicitly political.

In contemporary society, these movements are usually launched to promote or defend a cause through concerted collective action. The initiative of Jake Nickell, the founder of Threadless, provides an example of this type of movement.[2] Threadless is the website that revolutionized the T-shirt market on the Internet. Realizing that the creations of graphic designers – and therefore his own creations since he is in the profession himself – remained hidden secrets on the Internet because the attention they attracted was confined to mentions on discussion forums attracting little traffic, Nickell fought to make them more visible. His first idea was to introduce a contest for his fellow graphic artists that ended with the best designs being printed on T-shirts. Bit by bit, the movement slowly organized and grew to become a website on which graphic artists propose designs to the community, which then votes to decide which ones should be printed. Thus, in trying to find a way to defend his community's cause at the turn of the twenty-first century, Jake Nickell created the world's most successful business specializing in the creation of original T-shirts.

The first part of this chapter will examine what motivates individuals to defend a cause and join a movement. The second part will attempt to explain how to launch a movement and allow a community to emerge. Finally, the chapter will address the important issue of the transition from the community to the business that allows a movement created to defend a cause to become a start-up.

WHY ARE INDIVIDUALS TODAY ATTRACTED BY THE OPPORTUNITY TO DEFEND A CAUSE?

To understand why movements that promote or defend a cause have a powerful natural attraction today that allows them to mobilize people, it is necessary to make a detour and begin by examining the construction of identity in contemporary society. In the Western world today, the construction of identity is a process that never ceases to be renewed. People continually remake themselves – they are constantly reborn – through identity mechanisms that manifest their subjectivity. Not so long ago, Western reformers fought to overcome the limits to identity imposed by casts, by blood, by lineage, and by clans, and to ensure that human beings can live for themselves as free individual subjects by openly assuming the identities that define who they are. But identity is not something static and already given – it is something that comes into being and evolves as a fragile dynamic process. This construction of self is a tremendous opportunity for individuals because it gives them an ever-increasing number of capacities. However, these capacities come with additional duties and responsibilities; in particular, they force individuals to determine the meaning of their own lives – they give them the task of inventing themselves. Individuals can and must expose who they are by engaging in personal action that creates and reveals their own existence, their own difference, because the construction of self has become an ineluctable task. All individuals, no matter what their origins, must undertake the often difficult existential project of becoming a distinctive someone with a unique identity.

It is through social experience that the self develops the coherence no longer provided by 'the system' or by social norms. However, this coherence has limits and often takes the form of a struggle that manifests itself in three fundamental spheres: the sphere of primary sociality where love and affection are sought among family and friends; the sphere of secondary sociality where there is an expectation of civility and respect in furtive interactions with people encountered in public contexts (employees in government services, wait staff in bars and restaurants, hairdressers in beauty salons, etc.) and the sphere of the work world where individuals are tacitly encouraged to seek recognition, particularly when it is a question of making an effort to contribute to the productivity of a business.

Unfortunately, in contemporary society these three spheres of recognition no longer function adequately, and this can lead to the unsettling experience of 'recognition panic'. As far back as the 1980s, the need for identity consolidation was colliding with the liquefaction of work. Indeed, by the 1990s, it was clear that work could no longer provide people with a stable foundation for building their identity. Unemployment rates tend to be high, and even if people do find jobs, they can quickly lose them. The organizations where people work are constantly merging with other ones or even disappearing. In accordance with the diktats of strategists, the name of an organization can change several times over the course of a decade. Burn out and bore out destroy the value of the work experience. Remote work isolates people and cuts them off from contact with others.

This means that individuals must search outside of professional contexts for gratifying social experiences with the potential to fulfil their need to consolidate their identity. Suffering from identity instability that is provoked by the weakening of previous norms and social orientations as well as by difficult life events and disruptions, individuals find causes to defend that provide them with the means to (re)construct their identity. Indeed, in contemporary society, it is often this type of engagement that enables individuals to succeed in building an identity that is truly their own. Moreover, the effectiveness of this type of social engagement has more to do with horizontal recognition (from other persons associated with the cause) than with vertical recognition (from some higher authority). Occurring at the level of primary sociality, this recognition is embodied and tangible. As such, it stands in contrast to recognition at the level of secondary sociality, which tends to be disembodied and intangible. Numerous types of movements, ones with a wide variety of different goals, can contribute to the identity construction of individuals. In the past, people fought for a better future, but today they tend to defend causes that are less weighty and more local. The localness of causes restores the fabric of true community and makes people feel that they depend on other human beings, not on faraway bureaucracies or anonymous forces. They can be militants without believing in a glorious future for the world, and they can become intensely involved in a local cause without attempting to realize a utopian dream. Such movements do not have to be serious; indeed, a certain degree of playfulness is necessary to mobilize people today.

WHY DO PEOPLE TODAY JOIN A MOVEMENT TO DEFEND A CAUSE?

People today who make a commitment to defend a cause tend to be motivated by two main categories of objectives:

1. Objectives centred on improving the world.
2. Objectives centred on saving whatever can still be saved.

Improving the World

A legacy of utopian movements, the possibility of becoming an advocate committed to improving the world is a dimensional aspect of contemporary society with structural impacts. This is even evidenced in Silicon Valley where businesses never tire of repeating that their founders were initially motivated by a fundamental desire to improve the world! In the discourse of Big Tech, we never cease to hear that these firms help 'make the world a better place'. Thus, Facebook's initial goal was to 'make the world more open and connected', and it has recently stated that it wants to 'bring the world closer together'. Instagram says that it is 'about bringing you closer to the people and things you care about'. Hindsight allows us to see that the endless repetition of the phrase 'make the world a better place' by the owners of Big Tech serves to cover up platform capitalism and gross irresponsibility when it comes to the content that flows through these companies' networks. If it were true that the new information technologies could improve the world, then we should have seen this improvement long before now.

For causes and movements that have been able to bring people together instantly and that have had a real impact, it is necessary to find less impressive examples involving more limited ambitions. This was the perspective of American Internet entrepreneur Casey Fenton in 2003 when he framed the mission of Couchsurfing as an invitation to 'participate in creating a better world, one couch at a time'. Thus, the Couchsurfing movement makes an appeal to generosity. If people wish to attract travellers to their homes, then they must create a profile on the website and offer a couch, a bedroom, a hammock, a tent, a backyard, etc. In other words, the term 'Couchsurfing' makes literal reference to surfing from one couch to another one. For travellers, it is an opportunity, not only to discover a region, but also to learn about its inhabitants by staying at their homes. For hosts, it is an opportunity to meet new people and perhaps even to reciprocate the favour if they themselves make use of the website as travellers. In a way, Couchsurfing is to the accommodations sector what hitchhiking is to the tourist transportation sector. It has given rise to the hope that the world can be improved by the spirit of sharing and conviviality. The firm is able to operate thanks to the commitment of volunteer hosts in 232 countries and thanks to the work of numerous other volunteers who develop and maintain the website and who even make donations to the Couchsurfing association. As we will discuss in more detail below, this wonderful success story began a new chapter in 2011 when Casey Fenton decided to turn the association into a for-profit business, but one with social and environmental goals, which meant that Couchsurfing became a certified B Corp.[3] In 2011, the community that was created around the movement had 3 million members.

And there are other initiatives that have the goal of making the world a better place:

- Slow Food, created in Italy by Carlo Petrini in 1989, wants to create 'a world in which all people can access and enjoy food that is good for them, good for those who grow it and good for the planet'. The goal of this non-profit international movement is to mount an offensive against fast-food restaurants, pre-prepared dishes and industrial agriculture by encouraging citizens to become aware of how important it is to take into consideration the taste and the origin of food, and to do so out of respect for the environment. The organization 'believes that everyone has a fundamental right to the pleasure of quality food, and consequently the responsibility to protect the heritage of biodiversity, culture and knowledge that make this pleasure possible'.[4] Slow Food has inspired many similar movements, including Slow Fashion and Slow City.

- 'Together, let's build a better world by tackling the climate crisis!' is the rallying cry of Alternatiba,[5] a citizens' movement originally sponsored by Stéphane Hessel. Launched in France in 2013, the movement is inspired by two fundamental facts. First, climate change is accelerating. It now affects the poorest populations on the planet, and in the near future it will threaten life on earth. Therefore, it is necessary to act now to avoid reaching a threshold where climate crises become uncontrollable. Second, solutions exist and are already within reach. Alternatiba wants to make these solutions known and to reinforce and develop them so that the system can be changed.

- ShareTheMeal's 'Together, we can be the generation that ends global hunger' project revolves around a smartphone participative financing application that enables people to help in the struggle against hunger (United Nations World Food Programme).[6]

- The goal of Wanted Community[7] is 'to strengthen social cohesion in order to offer everyone the opportunity to act locally and build a more inclusive and sustainable society'. After an initial Facebook group was created in 2011 to exchange 'addresses and discuss tips for finding housing', its founders were overwhelmed by the movement of solidarity that it generated. In just a few years, this Facebook community became the most important one in France. The mutual aid and social cooperation can take various forms. There are groups such as the 'Maraudeurs by Wanted Community', which meets every Friday evening near the Austerlitz train station in Paris to provide help to homeless persons, and every day there are thousands of other efforts to offer a helping hand to people in need. In addition, a hundred volunteers called 'Wantediens' play an indispensable role by responding to the 6 million comments springing from an annual total of 1 million posts. In 2018, Facebook awarded Wanted Community $1 million for being the best virtual community in the world. The money helped make it possible to launch the first Wanted Café, where every day of the week free meals are offered to people in need. In December 2019, Wanted Community was actively present in 86 countries, including many outside France, and it had more than a million members.

Finally, it is important to note that marketers have understood the impact of the 'make the world a better place' formula. This is clear, for example, in the allusion made to this formula in an ad for Absolut vodka: 'Create a better tomorrow, tonight'. The director of global communications for the brand maintains that Absolut has always promoted the power of creativity as a way to foster progress in the world.[8]

Saving Whatever Can Still Be Saved

Our postmodern or even post-postmodern society is characterized by causes and in particular by ones where the goal is to save or protect a world in peril. Because of what sociologist Hartmut Rosa[9] has described as the 'acceleration of the acceleration' of change and because of the deconstruction of the world of earlier times, many causes are now 'retrotopian'[10] as opposed to utopian movements. Instead of striving to change the world, their goal is to save whatever remains of it. Promises for a brighter future have given way to dire predictions about potentially cataclysmic events and various types of catastrophic collapse. Today an apocalyptic mindset predominates, one that accentuates the retreat into the past and the valourization of the local to the detriment of progressive universalism. Sometimes there is even an attempt to preserve what was considered abhorrent during a previous era. This seems to be the case for the communist legacy of East Germany in the famous film *Goodbye Lenin*. Moreover, retrotopia has even led American actor David Hasselhof to go to the German capital to do everything in his power to preserve the Berlin Wall's longest surviving stretch.[11] Indeed, faced with the possibility that its remaining sections may be torn down to make way for a range of urban development projects, Berliners are mobilizing to save this despised symbol of the Cold War, and David Hasselhoff sees it as his duty to join them in their effort to protect what remains of the notorious wall.

A commitment to saving the planet animates many of the causes that are defended. 'Save the Arctic' is the rallying cry for the *Protect the Arctic* movement initiated by Greenpeace.[12] The Arctic regulates the climate of the entire earth, which means that saving the Arctic amounts to saving the earth. Such a cause can mobilize a great number of people, but other less pressing and less global causes also have supporters. The following examples of movements to defend a cause in France tend to involve a focus on revitalizing local customs and products:

- The struggle for the return of the bidet to French bathrooms. In contemporary France, bidets are seen as hopelessly old-fashioned. Yet this absurd rejection of them is dubious from a hygienic perspective according to France's neighbours in Italy and England, where they continue to be used, and it contributes to the ecological disaster caused by the overconsumption of toilet paper;

- Reviving funeral traditions that have disappeared. In the past, when someone in a French neighbourhood died, people put up in their windows black curtains into which they had sewed the initials of the deceased person. During the COVID-19 pandemic, some people recalled this lost tradition and tried to revive it in the face of high mortality rates. It seems clear that this was a way of compensating for the impossibility of gathering for funerals;

- The struggle for the return of French underwear! In the fight for the Frenchman's briefs at the beginning of the 2010s, Guillaume Gibault became the founder of the brand *Le Slip Français* (The French Underwear). An ardent defender of the Made in France cause, his goal is not only to defend the underwear, but also to support the workers who make it in a small factory in the South of France that first opened its doors 60 years ago. Adopting a patriotic national heritage tone and manifesting a kind of schoolboy enthusiasm in his communications, Guillaume Gibault mobilizes French citizens opposed to globalization: 'The issue of French underwear involves a veiled reference to the cliché about our unwavering national spirit that fights on against all odds with a kind of Charles de Gaulle *Vive la France!* attitude'.[13]

LAUNCHING A MOVEMENT AND BRINGING ABOUT THE EMERGENCE OF A COMMUNITY

Before attempting to persuade others, people themselves must have a strong desire to change something in the world. Such a desire is the starting point, not only of all political action, but also of any entrepreneurial project. It is always necessary to begin with an idea about how to make the world a little more beautiful, a little more just, a little nicer to live in, etc.

As a first step, a kind of manifesto must be written, one that consists of a public declaration in which the founder of the cause presents a problem and a well-thought-out action plan or policy position to address it. Today this declaration can take the form of a video or a social network post. The goal is to make people aware that this important issue exists. Ideally, an effective description of this issue should present it in both qualitative and quantitative terms. It is also important to indicate whether it is a world, a national or a local problem.

At the very beginning of the Slow Food movement discussed earlier, the group produced a manifesto. This founding declaration is celebrated every 10 years with a campaign like the one in 2019: '30 Years of the Slow Food Manifesto – Our Food, Our Planet, Our Future'. The manifesto denounces junk food, advocates the preservation of terroirs, local peasant agriculture and gastronomic legacies, and promotes food and taste education. It begins with the following statements:

—   Our century, which began and has developed under the insignia of industrial civilization, first invented the machine and then took it as its life model.
—   We are enslaved by speed and have all succumbed to the same insidious virus: *Fast Life*, which disrupts our habits, pervades the privacy of our homes and forces us to eat Fast Foods.
—   To be worthy of the name, *Homo Sapiens* should rid himself of speed before it reduces him to a species in danger of extinction.
—   A firm defence of quiet material pleasure is the only way to oppose the universal folly of *Fast Life*.[14]

The Slow Food manifesto defends a cause that brings together gastronomy and politics, but the manifesto of the Lomographic International Society is an excellent example of one that defends an aesthetic cause. With more than one million members from all over the globe, the Lomographic International Society[15] advocates a creative approach to photography as a means of communicating, absorbing and capturing the world. The movement was created in Vienna in 1992 when three students – Sally Bibawy, Matthias Fiegl and Wolfgang Stranzinger – came across a Lomo Kompakt Automat, a small enigmatic Russian camera. When they took random shots from the hip, sometimes using the viewfinder, they were astonished by the results. They had never seen such quality: the colours were vibrant and very saturated, the photos, nicely vignetted. They quickly created a manifesto with ten golden rules that were to guide the analogue photography movement as it attempted to come to grips with the rise of digital photography. Today, the Lomographic International Society defends the idea that 'the future is analogue'. Here are the 10 golden rules:

1. Take your camera everywhere you go.
2. Use it any time – day and night.
3. Lomography is not an interference in your life, but part of it.
4. Try the shot from the hip.
5. Approach the objects of your Lomographic desire as close as possible.
6. Don't think.
7. Be fast.
8. You don't have to know beforehand what you captured on film.
9. Afterwards either.
10. Don't worry about any rules.

When a movement is launched, it is possible to complete the manifesto by a petition. Alongside the petitions with an openly political character we find, in fact, petitions for the safeguard or maintenance of something considered important by a group of people. For instance, a petition has been addressed at the many Italians and non-Italians who love pizza all across the planet. The advocates of the cause named the 'The art of pizza'[16] fight for the Italian pizza to receive the prestigious and deserved UNESCO recognition and thus enter the 'Representative List of Intangible Cultural Heritage'.

The manifesto is the main tool for launching a movement and bringing about the emergence of a community. In particular through a petition, it is what makes people want to come together to talk about and defend the cause. Today, this is how a community is born, one that may seem unstable or even remain invisible to traditional sociology, but one that gives meaning to its members' lives – especially social meaning. It is here that entrepreneurs can play a notable role similar to the one played by enlightened entrepreneurs in Victorian England,[17] many of whom pursued commercial success while promoting social harmony at the same time through their concern for the construction of communities. However, Victorian entrepreneurs did not have the same conception of community as contemporary entrepreneurs. For them, a community was made up of a group of workers who were employed by a business, whereas for today's entrepreneurs, a community is a group of consumers.

Today, thanks to blogs and other types of social media, all it takes is one person to initiate a movement and rally a community to support a cause. In this respect, Emily Weiss and her blog *Into the Gloss* are a textbook case.[18] Born in Connecticut, Emily Weiss studied studio art at NYU, but while she was completing her degree, she also did an internship at *Teen Vogue*. Joining *Vogue* as a fashion assistant after she graduated, Emily learned the trade but became more interested in beauty products than in fashion. She became known to the American public through her appearance as a fashion intern in three episodes of the reality television series *The Hills*. She was a flawless young woman with impeccable style, but she had a difficult relationship with the cosmetic industry and its ever-present brands. It was at this point that she decided to turn her attention to the 'democratization of beauty'. In 2010, she launched her blog, *Into the Gloss*, as a movement to discuss beauty as it relates to the personal experiences and routines of real women instead of as a phenomenon connected to products and brands. The discussion on the blog quickly led to the emergence of a community of concerned women. With *Into the Gloss* taking a greater and greater place in her life, Emily Weiss finally decided that she should devote herself to it on a full-time basis. *Into The Gloss* is visited by millions of Internet users: it becomes not only a real encyclopaedia of the uses of 'beauty influencers', but also an international community of enthusiasts who do not hesitate to comment and exchange on their own uses below each portrait.

THE DIFFICULT TRANSITION TO THE
CREATION OF A BUSINESS

Once the cause has been defined and the manifesto written, the movement develops and the community increases in size. Then the difficult moment of transition arrives. How do you go from being an association anchored in primary sociality to being a start-up that operates on the market – where secondary sociality is the rule – without losing your community? Casey Fenton's Couchsurfing and Carlo Petrini's Slow Food appear to have failed in their efforts to make this transition, but the Lomographic International Society and Emily Weiss seem to have had more success in this respect.

When Couchsurfing was launched in 2003, it was a non-profit project with a website managed by volunteers, but in 2011 its founder Casey Fenton decided to transform it into a certified B corporation. He explained that he and his collaborators were proud to see their movement evolve into a business with a mission, that they would remain faithful to their fundamental values, and that 'Couchsurfing will never make you pay to host and surf'.[19] Most members of the community were unhappy about this change of status. They felt that Couchsurfing was taking advantage of people who just wanted to help each other out by offering a place to sleep for free. In their view, the founder was trying to make a profit from the kindness and the authenticity of people who were willing to share their homes with others. At first, many members fought to preserve the original spirit of Couchsurfing, but as time went by, considerable numbers of them left.

At first glance, Oscar Farinetti appears to be a fool who wants to save the world. A disciple of Carlo Petrini, the founder of Slow Food, he launched the Eataly store brand, whose mission is to promote good Italian food.[20] The concept, which lies somewhere between the supermarket, the gourmet grocery story and the restaurant, has conquered big cities all around the world. Oscar Farinetti pays scrupulous attention to the selection and the quality of the products sold, all of which are rigorously representative of the rich variety of culinary delights offered by the Italian countryside. In his view, Eataly owes its existence to the unparalleled biodiversity of Italy, a country with 538 varieties of olives and 1,200 varieties of grapes. Thus, it was a member of the Slow Food community who took up the task of giving a commercial dimension to the movement. Farinetti did so at his own expense, but many members of the community felt that their commitment to the cause had been betrayed by his action. It seemed to them that Farinetti was using the image of Slow Food to sell his products. This way of co-opting the work of the community was far from acceptable in the eyes of numerous members. As for Carlo Petrini, he has continued to develop the Slow Food movement and revived his friendship with Oscar Farinetti along the way.

The Lomographic International Society developed lomography, which became the name of a lucrative business enterprise in 1995. Since that time, Sally Bibawy, Matthias Fiegl and Wolfgang Stranzinger have been very careful not to talk publicly about business, never using terms such as 'sales' or 'revenue' with commercial connotations, even though the company sells thousands of Lomo cameras in a variety of different models. On the website, there is no reference to a for-profit business, no address for a head office. It is as if the community were self-managed and produced the cameras itself. A similar message is perceptible on social media. When Lomography launches a new project, it usually has recourse to participative financing by way of the Kickstarter platform. As a general rule, the reaction of the community consists in a show of massive support for the movement. The essential ambiguity of the relationship between the community and the business has been maintained for two decades, and identifying the boundaries between them continues to be difficult.

After the success of her blog *Into the Gloss*, Emily Weiss was advised by numerous experts to create a luxury brand, but she thought immediately of her community and its primary motivation. The founder explains[21] that she cannot find herself in the existing brands and that even when the products seduce her, the speeches remain too far from what she is. For her, a contemporary beauty brand must be digital, present where customers exchange, and must involve its consumers, integrating itself into their lifestyle. When Emily Weiss created Glossier in 2014, the design of every beauty product sold by her company was based on comments on her blog. She began by proposing four now iconic products: a face spray, a moisturizing cream, a lip balm and a skin tint. These were enormously successful in her community, and this allowed her to develop other product lines in the United States and all around the world.

The four cases presented here demonstrate the necessity of making a smooth transition to the business creation phase, one that does not disrupt or radically alter the community. The transformation of a movement into a start-up must not offend the non-commercial or even anti-commercial sensibility of the original community. The legitimacy of a start-up's founder is very important, but in itself it is never a sufficient guarantee that the transition will meet with the community's approval. If a brutal change occurs, the members of a community can turn against the founder who used to receive their full support as the spokesperson for their cause. This means that founder-entrepreneurs must subtly negotiate this key transitional stage with their communities. Moreover, if over a long period – as in the case of Couchsurfing and Slow Food – the members of the community have been allowed to foster anti-commercial attitudes and practices that make them averse to the contingencies of the business world, the transition can be excruciatingly difficult.

NOTES

1. Jacques T. Godbout & Alain C. Caille, *World of the Gift*, Montréal: McGill-Queen's Press-MQUP, 1998.

2. https://www.inc.com/ilya-pozin/how-to-start-a-business-without-really-trying.html

3. Michael O'Regan & Jaeyeon Choe. "Managing a non-profit hospitality platform conversion: The case of Couchsurfing.com." *Tourism Management Perspectives* 30, 138–146, 2019.

4. https://www.slowfood.com/press-release/the-united-nations-environment-programme-names-carlo-petrini-founder-of-the-slow-food-movement-a-champion-of-the-earth/

5. https://alternatiba.eu/

6. https://sharethemeal.org/en/

7. https://wanted.community/?lang=en

8. https://www.mynewsdesk.com/the-absolut-company/pressreleases/absolut-celebrates-the-power-of-creativity-in-new-global-create-a-better-tomorrow-tonight-campaign-2147434

9. Hartmut Rosa, *Alienation and Acceleration: Towards a Critical Theory of Late-Modern Temporality*, Aarhus: Aarhus University Press, 2010.

10. Zygmunt Bauman, *Retrotopia*, Cambridge: Polity Press, 2017.

11. https://www.theguardian.com/tv-and-radio/2013/mar/17/david-hasselhoff-returns-berlin-wall

12. https://www.greenpeace.org/usa/issues/protect-the-arctic/

13. https://start.lesechos.fr/innovations-startups/portraits-innovateurs/mais-quallais-je-faire-dans-cette-galere-1178395

14. The complete Slow Food Manifesto is available at https://vf63g1zsy1jqfwy46tx5qk6i-wpengine.netdna-ssl.com/wp-content/uploads/slow-food-manifesto.pdf

15. https://www.lomography.com/

16. https://www.change.org/p/proteggiamo-il-made-in-italy-la-pizza-come-patrimonio-unesco-2

17. Ian Bradley, *Enlightened Entrepreneurs*, London: Weidenfeld & Nicolson, 1987.

18. https://hashtagpaid.com/banknotes/how-an-influencer-built-the-most-recognizable-makeup-brand-on-instagram-the-glossier-success-story

19. Michael O'Regan & Jaeyeon Choe. "Managing a non-profit hospitality platform conversion: The case of Couchsurfing.com." *Tourism Management Perspectives* 30, 138–146, 2019.

20. https://www.eataly.com/us_en/manifesto/

21. https://hashtagpaid.com/banknotes/how-an-influencer-built-the-most-recognizable-makeup-brand-on-instagram-the-glossier-success-story

3

RECRUITING VOLUNTEERS

It is quite possible for the founder of a project to have an original idea that allows him or her to create a startup all alone. There are numerous ways in which a great idea can originate. It can have its source in expertise, professional experience, training that enables the development of indispensable competencies or even in special circumstances that provide the opportunity to launch a business project. However, investing in such a project is a tough decision with serious consequences – a decision that will monopolize the energy of the project founder for a long time. Therefore, to ensure that their projects move forward towards success, it is essential for entrepreneurs to surround themselves with the right people. Without a team, it is much more difficult, if not impossible, to overcome the complex challenges that lie ahead.

For many entrepreneurs, it is a question of mobilizing competent persons from the technical and managerial fields related to their project. This raises the difficult question of how to remunerate these persons with various competency profiles at a time when entrepreneurs do not necessarily have the financial means to do so. Should they promise these persons a future job? Should they offer them shares in the future firm or even a differed payment? This is where the idea of linking the project to the defence of a cause becomes relevant. If entrepreneurs have carefully argued for the urgency of the commitment to act, it should be possible for them to create an inner circle of volunteers who are prepared to participate in setting up the project by working on a part-time basis without pay. In this way, the project can benefit from the contribution of persons with various competencies (e.g. accounting skills and logistical know-how) without requiring the entrepreneur to make a financial investment.

Moreover, surrounding themselves with potential consumers or other persons who do not necessarily have technical or managerial competencies relevant to the project, but who are strongly motivated to support it, is also an excellent – although rarely used – way for entrepreneurs to move their projects forward. If entrepreneurs spend time developing a community around the cause that they want to defend, all the members of the movement can be considered potential contributors, and the earlier these members become involved in the project, the more loyal they will be.

The first section of this chapter will be devoted to the changes that led from the traditional associational form of volunteering to the current form, which is frequently referred to as 'leisure volunteering'. The second section will show that this new form of volunteering can have as its object an established or an emerging brand. The third section will specifically focus on the spontaneous or organized volunteering of individuals in support of a start-up project or brand. The chapter will conclude with a detailed presentation of the levers that entrepreneurs can use to develop and maintain this type of consumer volunteering.

VOLUNTEERING AND THE CHANGES
THAT IT HAS UNDERGONE

During the last 20 years, an ever-increasing number of associations have been created and volunteering has exploded. Almost one out of every three persons in France is a volunteer who gives up part of his or her own time to an associational organization. The majority of these persons work as volunteers in areas such as sports, culture, leisure activities or community action, but there are some who devote themselves to the defence of human rights or to causes such as climate change. For instance, a study indicates that around 20 million French citizens, that is, approximately 38% of French citizens aged 15 or more, freely give of their time to help others or to contribute to a cause.[1] More and more people say that their lives have meaning thanks to their commitment to do volunteer work outside of their jobs.

This form of volunteering is described as 'leisure volunteering'[2] because it is motivated by the personal interests of individuals, interests that may be related to social gatherings such as musical, artistic and sports events, or to sectors of activity such as tourism. Indeed, it develops around a wide range of activities that allow individuals to acquire human, social and cultural capital – types of capital that are especially significant for young persons entering the job market for the first time. Moreover, there is no necessary connection between leisure and idleness or superficiality. There is such a thing as 'serious leisure', leisure devoted to highly interesting and fulfilling activities that allow people to acquire experience, knowledge and competency. This is the case, for example, with Wwoof,[3] a worldwide movement to help men and women reconnect with the earth by volunteering to participate in organic farming practices. Wwoof's international eco-volunteering network puts volunteers into contact with ecological farms with environmentally friendly agricultural practices. The volunteers are hosted on the farms where they work in exchange for food and lodging. The farms that host these 'Wwoofers' are small agricultural businesses operating on a human scale, ones where families or collectives live and work. The Wwoofers help with the farm work and share the daily life of the hosts. Blurring the boundary between work tasks and activities outside of work, this volunteer programme gives participants the impression that the work they perform on the farms is not economic in nature. Volunteers come to see their interests and their fulfilling work tasks as merging with those of their hosts in an enchanting holiday-like setting.

Today volunteering is infused with a new vigour, but it has also taken on specific forms. The increase in the number of volunteers is occurring at the same time as the commitment to act is shifting towards customized activism. Volunteers tend to become involved when they can identify with causes and aspirations, when they see them as currently relevant, or when they know that they are fashionable. However, today's volunteers are not necessarily loyal to any specific organization. Pessimistic about what the future holds in store, they still believe in advocating for causes, but for them, it is a question of participating in concerted action to address one specific issue rather than trying to set up a utopia. As a result of these changes, the figure of the 'sad militant' – the professional activist dedicated to world revolution – has fallen into disrepute.

In contemporary society, volunteers are not looking for a cause that requires sustained engagement over a long period of time. Above all, they want their volunteering activities to give them a sense of fulfilment. In the past, activists had to adopt a posture of selflessness, but today it is a question of committing from a distance. The commitment to the cause is not total – it comes with a protective reserve and a certain adaptability. In other words, it is characterized by an everyday sociality with little evidence of a desire to enlist in the cause on a continuous basis. Above all, there is no desire for heavy responsibilities. As a result, these volunteers' commitment to act is precarious and unstable, and it involves changing processes of attachment to and detachment from associations and collectives.

The evidence suggests that in volunteering individuals are seeking the fulfilment and the sense of accomplishment that they no longer find in their professional lives. The role that volunteering plays in society has profoundly changed, and we are witnessing the development of new ways to be a volunteer.

FROM BRAND AMBASSADORS TO BRAND VOLUNTEERS

Surprisingly, some of these new volunteers accept to do unpaid work for brands. Among for-profit organizations, there is a growing tendency to have recourse to consumer-volunteers. These organizations are no longer merely relying on enthusiastic consumers or fans of their brand to develop word-of-mouth promotions and to evangelize other clients and customers; they are now calling on consumers to perform tasks within the framework of a volunteering programme organized by the business. Many consumers who want to spend less time working for the business that pays their wages or salary are willing to work for another one for free if it produces goods that they like or has a brand that pleases them. Some of these consumers go so far as to take a day off work or even to call in sick in order to be available to participate in these volunteering programmes!

These individuals are no longer simply consumers – they are devoted adepts or fans of a brand who are literally in love with it. This is just as true of Ducatists and Porschists as it is of Apple fans and AFOLS (*Adult Fans of Lego*). These consumers worship their favourite brand and use the Internet to meet together and organize collective action to support it. Thus, they work for the brand outside of any formal organization. Some businesses have seen this type of volunteering as something that can be organized around the goal of reducing production costs and giving their brand an aura. For example, Barilla, Decathlon and Fiat call on these passionate enthusiasts in the new approaches to collaborative marketing that they use for their respective brands: Mulino Bianco, Kalenji and Alfa Romeo. They invite these fans to participate in formal collaborative programmes as brand volunteers.[4] Up until recently, volunteering typically occurred at non-profit organizations, but we are now seeing for-profit organizations ask consumers to do unpaid work to help develop a brand. This is the case for Honda's *Next Door* programme (see Box 2).

Box 2. Honda's *Next Door* Programme.

At a time when the average age of new car buyers in France was steadily increasing, and when the customer experience at dealerships often left a lot to be desired, the Japanese car manufacturer Honda and its creative services agency Sid Lee put the company's sales campaign into the hands of passionate Honda drivers, asking them to play a starring role in the campaign by working from out of their homes.[5] In 2017, Honda France wanted to get the word out about its SUV product line with a focus on two models that had been launched a few years earlier – the 2015 HR-V and the 2011 CR-V – both of which had been well received on the market even though the SUV market segment where they were evolving presented challenges from both a communications and an innovation perspective. However, in addition to these market segment challenges, the Japanese car manufacturer also lacked the sales force of its competitors, having close to four times fewer dealerships in France than Renault and Citroën, and only about half as many as Fiat and Volkswagen.

Yet Honda had strong approval from its customers – who were willing to recommend the brand to anyone. It was the Sid Lee agency in Paris that came up with the idea of drawing on the communitarian dimension of this approval after looking into what was being said about the Japanese brand on social media. Indeed, the Net Promoter Score obtained by the brand, which was among the best scores for any category of product or business, confirmed that the community of customers had enormous potential as a source of strongly positive recommendations and therefore as the basis of a communications strategy. Thus the car manufacturer and its creative services agency decided to create a week-long volunteering programme in which Honda's fans could use their own homes as short-term dealerships for the brand. Without the passionate enthusiasm of Honda community members, such a project would never have been possible. Who could love a brand to the point of wanting to become an actual salesperson for it, simply out of passion, and without being paid? It is difficult to imagine very many people who would be willing to do this – except, of course, Honda fans.

In September 2017, Honda and Sid Lee identified about a dozen fans of the brand who had a home garage. For the week-long operation, the brand transformed these home garages into short-term dealerships where a completely new type of test drive was proposed to potential buyers. Walls were painted in Honda's colours; bright signs were installed; there was point of service advertising and there were CR-V and HR-V demonstrator vehicles on hand. Everything possible was done to recreate the atmosphere of a Honda dealership at the homes of the brand's fans. With characteristic passion, these fans donned a company shirt and a tie to embody the role played by salespersons at Honda dealerships. As the creative service agency points out: 'Nobody makes a better salesperson than a fan.'[6] The campaign was deployed on television, in newspapers and on social media. In particular, there was a film relating the story of Honda Volunteer #1 – a certain Jean-Baptiste, the French name for the biblical prophet John the Baptist! Reaching 16 million persons and bringing about 1,053 test drives in 6 days, the campaign was a resounding success that led to a 68% increase in Honda SUV sales in France the following month.

Similarly, Disney has a programme called the Disney Parks Mom Panel that brings together;

> *diverse and knowledgeable panelists [who] exude a passion for Disney and [who] have one goal in mind – to provide you with helpful tips and heartfelt advice so you can plan the family vacation of your dreams.*[7]

Every year, a demanding selection process is used to recruit fewer than twenty new panellists (in 2020, only 14 out of 10,000 candidates were recruited!) to collaborate with Disney. Extremely challenging, their work consists in answering questions throughout the year from people from their region who are planning a trip to a Disney Park. Yet a *New York Times* journalist who interviewed several Disney Park Moms states that most of them see their unpaid panellist position as a kind of a privilege that makes them feel like members of the 'Disney family'. Still, although these consumers make clear that they are very proud to participate in the volunteering programme set up by the multinational, the amount of negative reaction to the *New York Times* article on Disney panellists is striking. There are some who maintain that these panellists 'should be ashamed' to work for free for Disney. Others express continued anger at Disney and its appalling exploitation of the talent and the intelligence of these panellists.[8]

This commitment to work for free can be explained by the need for acknowledgement that torments almost everyone in contemporary society. When their jobs give them no opportunity to fulfil this need, people seek this fulfilment outside of the context of paid work. For example, they may take up hobbies or become volunteers. More and more people maintain that their lives have meaning thanks to their committed participation in activities outside of work that revolve around leisure volunteering in support of brands. These brand volunteers obtain so much intrinsic satisfaction from these activities that they do not seek any form of extrinsic satisfaction (pecuniary remuneration, price reductions, gifts, etc.). The most astonishing thing about their attitude towards brand volunteering is that they do not have the impression they are working. They do not feel as if they have been transformed into consumer-workers and they do not automatically refer to themselves as workers. In this respect, the refusal of brand volunteers to see their volunteering activities as work may point to the limits of sociological theories suggesting that businesses take advantage of their clients and customers by putting them to work. It may be the case that this notion of putting clients and customers to work is an invalid sociological interpretation of the observed reality. On the other hand, although brand volunteers may claim not to experience their volunteering activities as work, this is no proof that they are not in fact working.

BEING A VOLUNTEER FOR A START-UP BRAND

When it is a question of a new and completely unknown brand with no prior history and no immediate value for consumers, is it possible for brand volunteers to have the same degree of commitment? The answer is 'no' – unless these volunteers can be mobilized to defend a cause.

This type of mobilization is typified by Lomography, the brand originating with the Lomographic International Society that we discussed in Chapter 2. Defending a creative approach to analogue photography that highlights its connective value, the initiators of the Lomography movement used volunteers right from the beginning to diffuse the Lomographic spirit. Thus, in the largest cities in the world, they created LomoWalls inside or outside buildings on which photos taken with Lomo cameras by local community members were exhibited. As a complementary activity, Lomographic volunteers organized community parties that took the form of vernissages celebrating the local LomoWalls:

> *Two Lomography fans, Tom Ambrose, a University of Manchester student, and Monica Sagar, an Arden School of Theatre graduate and native Mancunian, have spent three weeks with the Lomography UK team carefully creating the masterpiece using over 1,000 different images of Manchester submitted by more than 500 people.*[9]

Introduced near the beginning of the Lomography movement, this tradition continues today even though the project has become more commercial. For example, in the Philippines in 2018, the International Lomography Society used the local Lomographic community's Facebook page to recruit ten volunteers to help create a LomoWall in Manila.[10] The recruitment message emphasized that the volunteers would be responsible, not only for posting the photos and assembling the LomoWall, but also for responding to a very large number of SMSs, emails and phone calls. For certain LomoWalls, the volunteers must defray some of the costs connected to creating them.

Consumer volunteering goes together well with participative financing. In 2007, Martin Dickie and James Watt decided to do something about the boring brands of beer that were dominating the market. They started a project to revitalize beer by associating it with the punk movement, just as had been done for rock music during the 1970s. Pooling their savings, they launched the project and in April 2007 BrewDog finished its first batch of beer. 'The beer scene is sick and we are the f**king doctors.' Their timing couldn't have been worse. A year later, the Great Recession hit. No one wanted to buy an unknown, hoppy, bitter brew:

> *We had to both move back in with our parents, because we couldn't afford to pay ourselves, which was fun at 24. And we did everything, the two of us, from filling bottles by hand to sleeping on sacks of malt on the floor', Watt says.*[11]

The turning point was in 2009 when they came up with *Equity for Punks* financing, a financing model that they described as antibusiness. Thanks to this participative financing programme, the cause of *punk beer* received the support of numerous punks and other fans of extreme beer. The idea was simple: by buying stock people become privileged members of the punk beer community. From the start, the Brewdog financing campaigns were extremely successful, and support from volunteers continued to grow as the years went by. The *Equity for Punks* programme has brought together thousands of punk beer members and raised tens of millions of euros! A windfall for Dickie and Watt that allows them to benefit from solid financial support for the development of bars, breweries, international exports and new products. Today, the community has more than 135,000 *Equity for Punks* investors around the world. According to Watt;

> *it's an amazing business model because we don't see them as investors ... they're advocates, they're ambassadors, they're on this journey with us. They're the heart and soul of our business.*[12]

Thanks to the *Equity for Punks* fundraising drives, Brewdog was able to launch bars, first in Aberdeen, then in Glasgow, Edinburgh and London. The company remained the fastest growing agri-food business in the United Kingdom for 7 consecutive years! It now has over 2,000 employees and more than hundred bars around the world.

The preceding examples highlight the determination of entrepreneurs to mobilize volunteers, but there are cases where volunteering is triggered automatically. Indeed, sometimes there is no need to call on volunteers because they show up on their own to defend the brand without being solicited. This is what happened two decades ago in the case of *Eingana,* a video game created by the French start-up EMG that allows players to navigate around the entire earth. Game demonstrations were organized in France at many of the stores owned and operated by the French retail giant *Fnac.* It was not *Fnac* or *Hachette,* the distributor of the game, that sent out the invitations to attend these demonstrations, but instead a teacher from South of France. At 53 years old, he had become a fan of the astonishing game that reconstitutes and modifies the earth's landscapes in accordance with the time of the day and the season. While the game is being played, the computer relies on averaged data contained in its memory. This allows the user to dive into the ocean to search for the Titanic, to face a snowstorm at the summit of Mont Blanc or to encounter one of the two hundred animal species in the game's repertory. Thus, the educational benefits of such a game are relatively important. 'I really admire the possibilities this game has – so much so I want to help EMG, the French firm that created it',[13] says the teacher who contacted a dozen fans of the game on the discussion forum of the website eingana.fr. Together they set up the demonstrations at the *Fnac* stores, including the one at Saint-Germain in Paris. The sales manager at EMG admitted that he was quickly overwhelmed by this group of unsolicited volunteers: 'Everything began with the forums where these enthusiasts were exchanging about their project. But we weren't the ones who set in motion the initiatives with the distributors.'[14] In fact, the founders of the game had put all their energy into designing *Eingana*, a project that had taken more than four years' work and investment, so they were very happy to see a group of self-declared volunteers take on the task of promoting it.

The case of the *Sezanettes* is another great illustration of spontaneous volunteering. *Sézane* is a women's fashion brand from France that was launched on the Internet by Morgane Sézalory in 2013.[15] The brand had more than 2 million Instagram followers in 2021. Its fans began by opening individual accounts on social media, particularly Instagram and Facebook, using revealing pseudonyms like 'mademoiselle_sezanette', 'sezane_lover' and 'sezanemonamour [sezanemylove]'. By posting photos of their purchases and their Sézane look, these fans attract more and more followers, mostly women, who are passionate about the brand. Some of them also take advantage of social media sites to resell items from previous collections. Facebook groups have been created, including 'Sezanettes DIY', which has more than 19,000 members.[16] This group is devoted to all the clothing alteration activities connected to the Sézane brand. Other groups of Sézane fans spend time on social media sites exchanging advice, information and tips. Sometimes they even transform these sites into veritable marketplaces.

The most impressive group is the *Sezanettes*, a group of women who define themselves as follows[17]:

> *Independent and without any political cant, Sezanettes will keep you informed of the best and the worst of the Sézane brand. Feel like joining the adventure? Send us your photos, your rants, your fashion favorites, your most beautiful Sézane looks, your exclusive info on the brand and its boutiques. In a word, share your experience!*

These groups have even organized a market for second-hand clothes where it is possible to buy, sell and exchange them, which must certainly please the founder of Sézane who made her debut on the Internet selling vintage items on eBay. These individual and collective initiatives, which are all independent from the brand, highlight the different forms of activism that consumer-ambassadors for online start-ups engage in. Ever since it first appeared, this activism has been shaking up codes of behaviour in every sector of activity. It is also interesting to note that these initiatives are in line with the values of the brand: solidarity (sharing, exchanging information) as well as the reduction of waste and the promotion of sustainable and responsible consumption (buying second-hand, doing it yourself). And volunteering can function without the founder having to intervene. In the case of EMG and Sézane, the founder had no direct communications whatsoever with the groups and activities managed by fans.

THE LEVERS OF VOLUNTEERING

Brand volunteers find the self-sacrifice that they make to perform volunteer tasks intrinsically satisfying, and they do not feel the need for any form of extrinsic satisfaction (gifts, rebates on products, financial remuneration, etc.). However, although self-sacrifice is at the heart of volunteer participation, it is a fragile reality that can easily disappear if the business fails to interact with volunteers adequately.

A business should not attempt to satisfy brand volunteers by treating them as consumers or try to motivate them as if they were employees. Instead, it should mobilize them through a collaborative programme based on the seven following levers:

- The business thanks and rewards volunteers for their efforts.

- It ensures that the competencies of each volunteer are put into play.

- It organizes the volunteer programme in a flexible way to adapt to each volunteer's preferred manner of participating.

- It fosters an emotional attachment to the programme and to the other volunteers.

- It makes explicit the moral signification of collective action.

- It respects each volunteer's contribution no matter what task he or she performs.

- It encourages volunteers to feel a sense of pride about participating in the programme.

The failure to integrate one of these seven levers can rapidly lead to the withdrawal of brand volunteers from the programme, and this withdrawal can result in a quantitative reduction in production (fewer volunteers, less effort) as well as a qualitative one (fewer relevant ideas, less involvement). The Fairtrade Town movement created a volunteer programme to promote the awarding of FT certification to regions and communities that actively endorse the sale of fair-trade goods, but it faced a revolt among the volunteers when some of them began questioning the moral signification of their involvement in the movement after discovering that large multinational corporations had been accepted as sponsors.[18]

Among the seven levers of volunteering, pride appears to be the most important one. Indeed, brand volunteers enjoy contributing to something they consider important and interesting, and having the opportunity to use and develop their talents and knowledge in activities that allow them to share with others. This enjoyment is linked to pride understood as the satisfaction of 'being a stakeholder', for being proud of something always involves having an emotional, a financial or a cultural investment in its success.

But this raises the following question: How can people be proud if they suspect that they are being exploited when they freely invest their time and effort. Researchers even suggest that consumer-workers may be doubly exploited when they collaborate with a brand for free. Thanks to their volunteer work, the brand increases its value and can charge a premium price for its products and services, and this directly impacts these consumer-workers who are the most enthusiastic consumers of these products and services. Moreover, the digitalization of exchanges tends to facilitate this type of exploitation of consumers. Without any safeguards against exploitation related to online production, as in the case of the collaborative online work done by Disney panellists, brand volunteering can quickly become alienating for consumer-workers. When this occurs, the business's lack of respect for the volunteers that it exploits and alienates stands in stark opposition to their pride. But brand volunteers say they fail to see the exploitation. This is explained by the fact that their commitment to the brand allows them to affirm their identity and develop competencies.

Should we not still conclude that this new approach poses a problem? It is worth asking whether businesses that call on volunteers are in breach of the law. As it turns out, they are in breach of the law, at least theoretically, in both France and the United States. Indeed, the American *Fair Labor Standards Act* explicitly states that volunteer work at a for-profit business is unlawful. Anyone working at a for-profit business must receive remuneration that is based on the time spent on the job, no matter what type of work is performed. However, businesses can claim that the time consumers spend doing volunteer work is insignificant compared with the normal amount of time employees spend working. A further difficulty is related to the development of remote work. Also called digital work, it remains largely invisible, raising the issue of how to identify or measure work done for free. How would it be possible to keep an accurate record of the time Disney panellists spend working as volunteers on the Internet?

These questions about the potential exploitation of volunteers and the potential illegality of certain approaches to brand volunteering must be put into perspective by taking into consideration the diversity of possible levels of involvement. A start-up can receive support from social media posts and exchanges that contribute to it collectively, with individual contributions absorbed into the overall collective effort. It can also receive the support of part-time quasi-employees who take charge of a designated task for many months and sometimes even for years. The development of remote work has multiplied these possibilities without the law being able to limit them, for in online contexts, it is difficult to differentiate with any great accuracy what should be considered leisure time from what should be considered work time. In any case, the impression that they are being exploited is not predominate among volunteers; on the contrary, they mostly feel a sense of pride. Exploitation only becomes an issue in crisis situations that make individual volunteers fully aware of what others are gaining from their contribution. When this occurs, volunteers leave behind the spirit of giving that is the basis of their commitment to volunteering and adopt a market-exchange mindset for which everything must be counted and calculated.

Today there is no longer a rigid opposition between volunteering and work as it is understood in the business world. Instead, the two combine. Volunteering is now so important that start-up projects are unthinkable without having recourse to this type of commitment. It is indispensable for motivating people to become the founding members of a brand community.

NOTES

1. https://www.francebenevolat.org/sites/default/files/DOCUMENTATION/ ETUDE_Evol%20b%C3%A9n%C3%A9volat%20associatif%20en%20 2019_DEF.pdf

2. Robert A. Stebbins, *Leisure and the Motive to Volunteer: Theories of Serious, Casual, and Project-based Leisure*, New York, NY: Palgrave Macmillan, 2015.

3. https://wwoof.net/

4. Bernard Cova, La Vie Sociale des Marques. Caen: EMS, 2017.

5. https://sidlee.com/en/work/honda/2018/honda-next-door

6. https://sidlee.com/en/work/honda/2018/honda-next-door

7. https://plandisney.disney.go.com/meet-the-panel/

8. https://www.nytimes.com/2020/01/08/travel/disney-parks-moms-panel.html

9. https://www.theguardian.com/uk/the-northerner/2012/aug/10/manchester-lomo-wall

10. https://www.facebook.com/lomographyphilippines/

11. https://www.forbes.com/sites/kristinstoller/2020/01/14/the-new-beer-barons-how-two-scottish-kids-turned-wild-flavors-crowdfunding-and-plenty-of-attitude-into-a-2-billion-business/

12. https://www.forbes.com/sites/kristinstoller/2020/01/14/the-new-beer-barons-how-two-scottish-kids-turned-wild-flavors-crowdfunding-and-plenty-of-attitude-into-a-2-billion-business/

13. https://www.strategies.fr/actualites/marques/r26035W/quand-le-client-se-fait-representant-benevole.html

14. https://www.strategies.fr/actualites/marques/r26035W/quand-le-client-se-fait-representant-benevole.html

15. https://fr.fashionnetwork.com/news/Sezane-avec-la-certification-b-corp-morgane-sezalory-veut-s-affirmer-en-leader-du-renouveau-du-secteur,1353625.html

16. https://www.facebook.com/groups/583616945901990/

17. https://www.instagram.com/sezanettes/?hl=fr

18. Anthony Samuel, Ken Peattie, & Bob Doherty, "Expanding the boundaries of brand communities: The case of Fairtrade Towns." *European Journal of Marketing* 52(3/4), 758–782, 2018.

4

ENCOURAGING INTERACTIONS AND SHARING STORIES

When project founders think about encouraging interactions, what they are often – indeed, too often – wondering is how to influence people, especially online where it is easier to create a buzz. Efforts to wield a more direct influence tend, on the other hand, not to work nearly as well. The better option is to support interactions through community activities that foster both engagement and a sense of loyalty, that is, to recognize that a community-based approach is an integral part of any and all interactions between consumers. To repeat, it is essential that community members be provided with as many opportunities as possible for offline and online interaction.

The proposal here is not that project founders be viewed as a kind of relational nuclei but instead as support systems brokering connectivity between individuals united in their support of a cause. Founders will continue to act and communicate on their own behalf but should be doing this in pursuit of a single objective – ensuring that future community members have things they want to discuss together. The type of online platform being used towards this end is therefore less important than the type of story being told. Of course, it often transpires that project founders looking to recruit members post their more charming stories on Facebook or TikTok while using YouTube or podcasts for more intimate topics.

More importantly, however, they need to look beyond this particular level of intervention to try and get other people to tell their own stories – and histories – both online and offline.

Above and beyond this historical (and indeed, storytelling) aspect, project leaders seeking to encourage interaction within their communities have at their disposal many other resources – tools that have become popular again because of everything that is happening on social networks. Hashtag-type rallying cries have proven themselves very effective in uniting heretofore divided populations; gamers clearly battle one another because they enjoy networking; and even crowdfunding can be used as a powerful lever for interaction.

The first section of this chapter introduces an alternative to traditional marketing and branding models, one based on brands' narrative power. The second section demonstrates how the narrative put forward by project founders might provide fodder for discussion and interaction, first during a new activity's start-up phase and then when it starts consolidating. The third details how business founders can develop rallying cries capable of having an impact not only on their own communities but also beyond. The chapter concludes with examples where gamer battles or crowdfunding have proven to be particularly effective in sparking interaction.

A BRAND MODEL NAMED N.A.M.E.

Project founders must nourish their brands from the very outset, whether this means having the brand represent a movement, a company or the two combined. By so doing, they are developing materials that a community – and indeed the rest of society – will then be able to appropriate and discuss. Stephen Brown – has used the Harry Potter[1] saga to show how brands tell stories, many of which are tales redolent of others told by the likes of the Grimm brothers. This phenomenon might be referred to as a brand's narrative power. Brown drew upon this example to imagine a model capable of guiding founders throughout their projects' emergence phases, one he entitled N.A.M.E., an acronym that stands for Narrative, Ambiguity, Mystery and Entertainment.

Project founders working in these four dimensions can avoid some of the traps found within so-called rational communication, where the goal is to convince, influence and produce a communication sparking word-of-mouth. This model can be illustrated by the way in which the late Austrian entrepreneur Dietrich Mateschitz launched the Red Bull brand, gaining global fame with his energy drink concocted out of taurine, caffeine, sparkling water and sugar. Founded in 1984 and marketed in 1987, Red Bull is largely inspired from an Asian energy drink that Mateschitz discovered during a trip to Thailand. The fact that the brand is available today in more than 165 countries (with a whopping 7.5 billion units having been sold in 2020) is all the more impressive given its relatively arduous early years – a challenge that Mateschitz would subsequently use to create a very specific narrative (and let others tell very pointed stories) about how he did not allow himself to be discouraged by these teething problems. Indeed, the way he talks about his early problems today is to say that, quite the contrary, what he wanted to do all along was to sell a brand that is ambivalent, which school principals will not like but which pupils will demand to see in their lunch halls.

N for Narrative: Stories Instead of Histories

Some of the early challenges that Red Bull faced included merciless consumer panel product tests, which culminated in an initial massive rejection. Mateschitz's way of representing these experiences has been to claim that 'No other new product has ever failed this convincingly'.[2] The drink's colour seemed very unappetizing, with many testers disgusted by the way it stuck in their mouths and the bitter taste it left behind, like cough syrup. Nor did Red Bull's famous 'stimulates the mind and body' strapline get much traction. All in all, the initial feedback was negative, and it was something that Mateschitz struggled with at the time. The recurring narrative today, however, is quite different. The myth has turned into a tale that is all the more intriguing because of the pain its hero (Mateschitz) suffered in the early years. Even though he often insists that the period following the initial product tests 'were the three worst years of his life', Red Bull has had the good fortune that, alongside its official story, the brand has also developed a slew of other tales told by the people who had originally opposed the product – a body of work that has done more for the nascent brand than the world's best advertising campaign could ever have done. In reality, the European and North American regulatory and public health bodies both moved very quickly at first to raise questions about the product's potential noxiousness. By so doing, however, they were unintentionally triggering a word-of-mouth focused as much on the product's upsides as on its dangers. On 16 July 2008, for example, French Health Minister Roselyne Bachelot advised parents in that country to boycott Red Bull, castigating it as 'a drink that has no energy value (…), no nutritional interest but which can be seriously harmful'.[3] This statement (broadcast on France's LCI news channel) triggered a wave of discussions in French families and among teenagers – but one that benefitted Mateschitz since the many calls to boycott Red Bull (often emanating from parent associations) would ultimately become part of its own narrative. In the end, the Red Bull brand was actually strengthened by the contradictions between all the stories being told about it, even before being licensed for sale in France.

A for Ambiguity: Contradiction Instead of a Coherent Positioning

Whereas some may find Red Bull uninteresting, others will say that 'it gives you wings', especially when mixed with vodka, a combination that supposedly lets people dance all night long. Highly enriched with taurine and caffeine, Red Bull can propel people through a physically draining day, explaining why it is referred to as an energy drink. One IT consultant responding to a call for contributions on the French Le Monde's website – and someone describing himself as a heavy Red Bull drinker since the age of 18 years – explained that he would drink one can every night so he would be able to 'sit in front of a screen coding sixteen hours a day'.[4] Indeed, when taken together with cannabis, he felt that 'it put [him] into a trance-like state' where he could keep going until 5 or 6 a.m. Indeed, many young people do view Red Bull as a pseudo-narcotic, albeit something much less toxic than drugs like amphetamines or ecstasy. The company, on the other hand, depicts the product as a dietary supplement that is clearly no substitute for a normal, varied diet but which can – as the name suggests – complement a traditional meal. There is clearly some definition ambiguity here regarding whether Red Bull is a drink; a different kind of substance but one that is innocuous; a food supplement; a trendy cocktail mixer; or indeed, a pseudo-narcotic. There is no single answer to this. The end result is that instead of having a unique selling proposal, Red Bull is clouded in uncertainty, a state of affairs that actually benefits the brand since everyone defines it whichever way they like.

M for Mystery: A Permanent Grey Area Instead of Full Transparency

The best way to sustain the torrent of stories that people tell themselves about Red Bull – and to give voice to these tales – is by preserving their mysteriousness. The ingredients that go into Red Bull – most famously, the 'taurine' that it uses – receive a great deal of scrutiny (much in the same way as people question what goes into Coca Cola or Nutella). Indeed, it is because of the oddities of the brew that the product usually takes so much time to complete health approval processes (five years in Germany, for instance, and more than 12 years in France). Mateschitz long refused to publish the product formula, allowing the rumour to spread that taurine is a substance extracted from bull sperm or bile and in turn causing some to view Red Bull as an alternative to Viagra. By going out of his way not to deny these allegations, what he was actually doing was fuelling people's fantasies. When asked if it were true that Red Bull contains a juiced concentrate of bull testicles (sic), he replied in the negative but immediately went on to add that 'I always have to fly to Pamplona to source bull's testicles',[5] thereby implying that the purpose of his visits to this famous bullfighting city was to stock up on basic ingredients. Of course, each can of Red Bull is legally obliged to list its contents: carbonated water;

sucrose; glucose; acidity regulators (sodium carbonates, magnesium carbonate); acidifier (citric acid); taurine (0.4%); caffeine (0.03%); vitamins (niacin, pantothenic acid, B6, B12); flavours; and colourings (caramel, riboflavin). Even so, many people continue to obsess about the inconsequential 0.4% represented by the mysterious 'taurine', which is in actual fact nothing other than an amino acid naturally found in most animal and human tissues. It is a purely synthetic substance that pharmaceutical companies manufacture. Its confusing name comes from the Latin word *Taurus*, having been first identified in 1827 in oxen bile.

E for Entertainment: Giving Consumers the Pleasure of Talking About It

Red Bull is well-known for its big investment in sports like Formula 1 car racing, and for the spectacular competitions it also organizes, including the Red Bull Cliff Diving (an extreme sport), the Red Bull Crashed Ice (a dangerous skating race), the Red Bull Air Race (an aerobatics competition) or the Red Bull Wake of Steel (where contestants wakeboard on the wreck of an old cargo ship). The sum total of this sports entertainment accounts for around 30% of Red Bull's total current spend. What is less known is that Red Bull had initially been involved in putting together much cheaper tournaments, including one-on-one street ball (basketball) in prisoner yards, as well as paper plane competitions. For a few years from 1992 onwards, most of Red Bull's entertainment efforts revolved around Flugtag[6] events where teams of competitors would make human-powered flying machines and then try to fly them. The brand did something similar in 2000 when it launched cart racing. Note how easy it was to take part in these Red Bull Soap Box races since the only thing that contestants – teams of four comprising one driver, one co-driver and two pushers – needed was a safe engineless vehicle that they would design and make themselves in accordance with certain very precise specifications (width of less than 2m; length of less than 5m; and empty weight of less than 80kg). Some races, like the annual event organized in Paris, would attract up to 40,000 spectators, translating into an avalanche of hilarious photos and videos then being shared on social networks.[7] In this way – and despite its small budget – Red Bull succeeded very quickly in associating its brand with entertainment material.

The Red Bull example shows the different ways that entrepreneurs can foster on- and offline interactions surrounding their brands – and be highly successful using very unconventional branding approaches. There is much to be learned from Dietrich Mateschitz's attitude that a modus operandi of this kind is not inherently dangerous since all that counts is that interactions occur. Of course, when Mateschitz was expressing this view during the 2000s, he was probably not thinking about the possibility of having to contend one day with a rallying cry attacking his brand. Yet this is what happened in September 2020 when Thai anti-government student protestors spread the hashtag #BoycottRedBull, angered by the impunity enjoyed by one of the heirs to the brand after being involved in a fatal accident. Up until that point, this leading energy drink brand had been a source of great national pride in Thailand.[8] Afterwards, it became the symbol of all kinds of inequities that the anti-government movement was trying to highlight in general. In turn, this would turn into yet another yarn, this time about a brand that was already established and could therefore no longer be considered emergent.

AUTHENTIC LIFE STORIES

Consumers are generally on the lookout for great stories to swap and share. Where this relates to a new company or creation, they tend to enjoy tales about its chaotic journey and the different stages thereof – akin to the sort of trajectory that Red Bull and Dietrich Mateschitz experienced. What people look for and find in these yarns is the exact opposite of the strategic profit maximization-oriented approach characterizing and structuring much modern life. They seek and find more of an antistructure, in the sense given to this term by the anthropologist Victor Turner.[9] What they want is a world that is the reverse of the one in which they live.

Consumers who are fans of this inverted world, with its rejection of economic primacy, urbanization and artificialized living, generally want to be able to laud its authenticity – a need that often boils down to looking for things that are extraneous to the market system and/or do not seem commercial in nature. This reflects their mistrust and suspicion of inauthenticity, meaning anything that is too obviously beholden to the market economy and/or seems like economic opportunism. Of course, people might still admire, for instance, top chefs using their restaurant businesses to accumulate great wealth. But that is because they are viewed as authentic individuals whose actions are driven first and foremost by a sense of vocation. Consumers not only do not begrudge the money they make (indeed, quite the contrary) but often consider the very topic of remuneration to be secondary in these cases.

The contemporary quest for authenticity tends to revolve around people's perception of the real intentions of anyone trying to found a movement or company, to wit, the things that make project founders seem authentic are the things they do without ulterior strategic motives.[10] The requirement here is therefore that they be viewed as acting more out of a sense of vocation than for commercial expediency purposes. This translates online into users browsing for stories about authentic lives, ones spent outside the world of trade or at the very least on its margins. If someone has also suffered a little and their life journey is strewn with pitfalls, he or she becomes even more authentic. This applies to singers, artists, influencers and all founders.

The case of Justine Hutteau, founder of the cosmetics brand 'Respire', is symptomatic of this trend. Everything started for her with the discovery of a disturbing health problem. The way she tells her story[11] is that,

> I was diagnosed with a benign tumour in my chest and started wondering about all my daily hygiene products, including deodorants, quickly making a connection due to the fact that the tumour was located under my right armpit. I started going through everything and soon focused on my deodorant ingredients, discovering that antiperspirants often contain aluminium salts, and that other, more traditional products in this category also contain endocrine disruptors. So I then started looking for something

that was highly rated [for safety] but was also very effective, since I'm such a sporty person. Plus I wanted it to be something where I'd have complete faith in the product narrative. And what I discovered is that there were no such products around! So in the end, I decided to create one.

Hutteau's story not only justified her interest in cosmetics but also legitimized the war she decided to wage against the harmful deodorants being sold at the time. More specifically, she focused on her product's composition, given the often controversial and sometimes dangerous ingredients that deodorants were using. The problem was finding a product that was both unambiguous yet effective enough to be useful to an athlete. An entire movement was born out of her insight, starting with the sports community but then followed, more broadly, by the many women who shared her health concerns. Another way of looking at this is that the Respire brand was born out of a movement that existed to support Hutteau. A few online voices would criticize what some called a 'benign' tumour being instrumentalized to develop an authenticity narrative. In their opinion, this indicated that the painful episode Hutteau had experienced was little more than a platform for a strategic intention that she was possibly already fomenting. Even so, it is worth noting the existence of a category of stories talking about the difficult journeys some people have made, including accidents or instances of harassment they may have suffered. One example is Marie Lopez, aka the YouTuber Enjoy Phoenix, who started posting videos online when recounting the harassment that she had been suffering for a whole year at school. Having charmed viewers with emotions but also humour, Lopez is idolized today by the many young girls who cherish her beauty tips.

Authenticity can go well beyond initiation stories, however, with many of today's YouTubers, for instance, finding authenticity in the closeness they feel to their followers. In addition to their millions of regular viewers, they often feel that it is possible to further influence their young audience by using straight talk, discussing their emotions and experiences – conversing all the while as if they were simply chatting with their sisters, brothers or friends. YouTubers entertain a very direct relationship with their community.

Some even like to stroll around the towns where they live and take selfies with fans. Others organize regular live meetups with subscribers. Above all, YouTubers are stars who do not look like stars, meaning for instance that they'll never talk about how much money they make. They try at all costs to remain 'normal youth' in the eyes of the audience, as if they were nothing more than simple high school students still living with their parents and scoffing at 'the system'. YouTubers have fully understood that their personal appeal – much like the attractiveness of the things they say – resides in their authenticity, that is, their being positioned outside the system and within the antistructure. Business founders giving off the impression that they are liberated and authentic, disinterested in marketing strategy.

Authenticity also runs throughout the simple stories that people like to tell about parties they went to with friends and following which they came up with a new product idea. An example is a tale that ended up revolutionizing the way Quebeckers use the word 'pocket'. One evening, Anthony Vendrame was at a gathering with a group of friends when he suddenly realized that he really liked the pocket on a T-shirt worn by his friend Pierre-Olivier, whose mother Josée had sewn a hamburger pattern onto a cotton jersey characterized otherwise by its minimalist design. The next day, Anthony bought some fabric and asked Josée to sew pockets onto a few plain T-shirts he had in his wardrobe. After that, every outing with Pierre-Olivier and his brother became an occasion for wearing different pockets, intriguing the friends they would meet around Montreal, with more and more of them wanting to get their own personalized pocket T-shirt. This is how Anthony recorded his first orders before even developing any entrepreneurial intentions. Starting with bits of fabric that he bought here and there, Anthony – now a student at HEC Montreal – would initially sell one T-shirt for $20 and two for $30, viewing the whole project mainly as a way of having fun and cashing in their silliness. And in fact, once the autumn semester began he spent less time on T-shirts, largely because his early fans seemingly had no interest in dealing with a real business. The story could have easily ended were it not for a decision that Anthony made the following January to team up with two friends and start a company that would ultimately

be called Poches & Fils.[12] The new venture moved quickly onto
Facebook to publicize its pocket products and, just as importantly,
to foster a brand community comprised mainly of top athletes
from the University of Montreal. The second move was to build
a website enabling secure transactions. As the company grew, its
founders began recruiting volunteers from their circles of friends,
asking them to manufacture pockets for piece-rate pay – labour
costs that were (alongside equipment costs and a modest rent for
the premises) the only significant outlays that the start-up had to
make at first. Each of these actions became fodder for stories that
were then shared across Anthony's Quebec fan community – with
March 2021 numbers reaching 102,000 on Facebook, 57,000 on
Instagram, 10,000 on TikTok and 3,000 on LinkedIn, all in addition to 25,000 direct email contacts.

Launching movements or start-ups becomes easier when accompanied by stories speaking to the authenticity of the founders, who
must also remain vigilant afterwards to avoid excess commercial-
ism or opportunism and nip in the bud any accusation of inauthenticity. For people to continue telling a tale, it must offer a modicum
of charm. If not, the social network narrative will be much less
effusive, that is, contain more criticism. One charming story told
on several forums (including the *Wall Street Journal*[13]) about Portland Oregon's Langlitz family and their eponymous jacket brand
shows how consumers' quest for authenticity can structure a company's entire life. Langlitz produces the same number of black
leather jackets a day as it did 60 years ago, to wit, six units, despite
their garment having become a must-have item over this stretch
of time. Today it is considered the Rolls-Royce of products in its
category, with a reputation that has spread from West Coast pris-
ons, biker bars and other Hells Angels landmarks to the offices of
the world's leading multinationals. At the same time, the production process has not changed one iota. Langlitz refuses to make
more than 1,600 units a year, including jackets and trousers. The
end result is an average waiting time of seven months, a delay that
neither fame nor bribes can shorten. According to production manager Thomas Schoen, 'I've gotten in arguments with plenty of guys
who have offered me a $100 tip to make a jacket faster … When I
say no, they've gone storming out of the door'.[14] Langlitz's modus

operandi has intrigued many North American management specialists, like James Rogers, an A.T. Kearney specialist working out of Chicago, impressed by the 'It's pretty unusual behaviour. In this country, we are trained to maximize our lifestyles all the time'.[15] The reason for this is that the family members who own and manage the brand are afraid that reckless growth will disrupt the peaceful atmosphere characterizing their small, 15-person company. As warned by David Hansen, a Langlitz manager living in a modest Portland suburban house with his wife, daughter of the late founder Ross Langlitz, 'If we grew, we'd have to work on weekends'.

This jacket example is a perfect illustration of the connection that exists between the authenticity of a product and the authentic vocation of its founders, well after the launch phase has finished. A product will be considered all the more authentic when it is not manufactured for commercial expansion purposes but because it is viewed as a representation of the founder-entrepreneur's true vocation rather than the business activity of some professional manager. In this one instance, jackets were viewed less as a typical modern business and more as the doings of a traditional family whose success had been achieved without prioritizing capital accumulation. Once again, it is by operating on the edges of a world otherwise structured by capitalist and commercial opportunism that a business founder creates material nurturing the stories that will be told about his or her authenticity.

ONLINE RALLYING CRIES AND HASHTAGS

Stories may be powerful tools for engaging members of a given community (and converting others to the cause that it is supporting) but there is also a more ancestral and primal way of achieving the same end, namely raising a rallying cry. Historical anthropology has revealed the importance of such cries in getting tribes and clans to move beyond whatever rituals they already share. One Scottish example from the late Middle Ages is the way each clan had its own tartan cloth but also rallying cry (or slogan), with the combination of the two reaffirming the collective identity of members going into battle. Similarly, French navy, infantry and artillery military personnel have a habit of shouting out 'By the grace of God, long live the colonial army' when attending a ceremony or meeting, traditionally signalled by the longest serving officer among the most senior ones present. It is a rallying cry that originated in the early years of the twentieth century when one Charles de Foucauld, isolated for a number of weeks in the midst of a local rebellion, glimpsed the arrival of a relief column composed of a company of colonial troops. The legend is that de Foucauld then fell to his knees, clasping his hands together and uttering these words of prayer. All in all, rallying cries are always a condensation of stories and values capable of instantaneously mobilizing the members of a community.

Today's rallying cry is the hashtag, which can reasonably be equated with a movement slogan. Digital rallying cries such as '#VegasStrong' was tweeted and retweeted a total of 92,347 times over a six-day period following the mass shooting that occurred in Las Vegas on 1 October 2017.[16] During the days following this terrible event, the Las Vegas community used the rallying cry 'Vegas Strong' to make clear that the event would serve as a reminder of the strength of the city. The choice of words is therefore paramount and must convey meaning. One counter-example is an attempt made by French health service officials to launch a #JaimemonCHU ('I love my hospital') hashtag, a clumsy expression with little resonance. In general, institutionalized hashtags rarely succeed. Much more effective are heartfelt exclamations initially acknowledged for their spontaneity before being instrumentalized as a way of organizing support. Some of the better-known hashtags to have turned into digital rallying cries in recent years include #BlackLivesMatter, following the deaths of a number of black Americans killed by police officers; #OccupyWallStreet, formulated by a movement of indignant American denouncing abusive capitalism and #JeSuisCharlie, which was retweeted more than five million times in the two days following the 7 January 2015 attack in Paris on the satirical newspaper, *Charlie Hebdo*.

In the absence of a hashtag, it is (almost) impossible nowadays to inspire virtual gatherings defending a theme or cause. Hashtags are sometimes simple cries from the heart; on other occasions, they are tools that activists wield knowingly; and just as often, they can be analyzed as little more than an effective way of rallying a community. One example is the hashtag #OscarsSoWhite,[17] a viral rallying cry aimed at promoting diversity in Hollywood. Created in 2015 by April Reign to denounce the dearth of people of colour among the celebrities nominated for that year's Oscars, it would remain relevant well beyond 2020, in part due to the lack of palpable progress in this domain. Reign, working as a business lawyer in January 2015, may have initially started the #OscarsSoWhite movement on Twitter but within a few short hours its effects would be felt on Hollywood's most prestigious film awards ceremony. Indeed, a simple message sent by just one person in Washington – reacting to the fact that the Oscar nominees were all white – took very little time to go all around the world. Years later, the hashtag would remain the rallying cry of people calling for greater diversity both at the Oscars and more broadly across the entertainment industry. It is specifically reactivated on social networks whenever a lack of diversity becomes flagrant, as happened again at the 2020 Oscars ceremony when all but one of the actors and actresses shortlisted for awards were white.

Niche hashtags are very different from mass formulations (like #Love, #Covid19, #queenelizabeth and #MeToo), but they remain very powerful. Despite their lesser popularity, specific hashtags make it possible to reach smaller communities precisely because they speak to very specific themes. It is what influencers do when they create their own hashtag to represent their movement or brand. They can reuse the hashtag in each of their posts while also encouraging subscribers to insert it into their own contents in order to encourage greater interaction.

Red Bull has also understood how a hashtag can mobilize a community of consumers. Inspired by a photo that a consumer had posted, Red Bull invited community members to stage a scene featuring their favourite canned drink and then share the photo adorned with the hashtag #PutACanOnIt.[18] Posts ranged from a motorcycle fitted with Red Bull can wheels to an optical effect that made it seem like a gigantic can was being hauled around by 20 people. A total of nearly 10,000 photos would end up being shared within a few months. Ninety-nine percent of the posts containing the hashtag were uploaded by consumers themselves, with many displaying great creativity. Similarly, the Canadian sportswear and fashion brand Lululemon – which came out of the yoga movement about 20 years ago – uses the hashtag #TheSweatLife to encourage its community to adopt a healthy lifestyle by practicing sports, especially yoga. The strategy is to strengthen the brand's ties to its customers. This starts with classes being held in Lululemon stores. Every year the company also organizes a one-day Sweatlife Festival featuring all kinds of classes, yoga coaching and personal development workshops. The hashtag #TheSweatLife increases word-of-mouth about all these events within the community. More broadly, most if not all start-up founders find it beneficial to rally their own community members using hashtags.

BATTLES AND JACKPOT FUNDRAISERS

Popularized by 'The Voice', a show that goes out on TV, battles (such as gaming jousts and other types of challenges or contests) are a powerful way of sparking interaction between community members, usually organized in this case into teams. The programme began as a competition between two hip-hop artists, with either a jury or the audience voting on the winner. It evolved into hip-hop team battles, a kind of event (and attitude) that would soon be adopted *en masse* by social networks. Instagram has even launched a 'Challenge' sticker where friends are given an opportunity to challenge one another. The purpose is to help app users encourage followers to participate in visual contests, thereby generating greater community engagement on Instagram. It is a feature reminiscent of the challenges found on TikTok (most famously, the #dontrushchallenge and #quarantine-pillowchallenge), which renews these events regularly to encourage community adoption and sharing. The preferred formats for sparking community member interaction are challenges involving videos triggering a rapid snowball effect once they are posted. Each participant spontaneously dares other users to take up the challenge. The greater the number of participants, the more visible the challenge becomes. Moreover, the challenges' viral nature boost a brand's visibility immediately once it becomes clearly associated with them. One example is the French La Redoute Challenge launched on TikTok in August 2020.[19] Assuming the form of a digital casting process reserved for teenagers between the ages of 13 and 18 years, it let participants express a full range of individual creativities and by so doing broadcast the digital campaign the brand was running in this famous French sales catalogue. All participants had to do was film a video featuring some kind of clothing-themed choreography backed by a specific song. A bespoke page was also created on TikTok carrying the hashtag #LaRedouteChallenge. As explained by the challenge organizer, 'There were no real barriers to entry; we were simply asking them to do what they usually do, producing the kinds of videos that they were already watching on the platform'.[20] The results were stunning with more than 100,000 videos being produced and a whopping 200 million views. Having said that, it is not because people take part in this kind of challenge that they automatically belong to a community of LaRedoute enthusiasts.

In a completely different vein and targeting a very different audience, online jackpot fundraisers have also demonstrated an ability to mobilize community members. Intended to facilitate crowdfunding, common pools of money accumulated in this way have become quite commonplace among young and old (and large or small) audiences alike. The aims include gift-giving among friends, project launches and solidarity fundraisers. Yet above and beyond this crowdfunding aspect, financial pooling encourages interaction by making it very clear why people should support a given cause or movement. It is also easy getting an online fundraiser that is being cleverly supported on social media to go viral.

Start-ups use these tools as a way of getting people to express and share their passion. In spring 2020, for instance, the B.R.A.I.N Escape Game – created in 2017 and run out of the town of Mondeville near Caen in France – used a prize pool for these purposes, something the founders talked about in the following terms[21]:

> *Allan and Anaïs started the project and were soon joined by Maxime, the first hire and an escape game fanatic. Subsequent recruits included David, and Maxence, the latter a very promising young employee. Government Covid restrictions then meant that the company had to shut down (until the lockdowns were lifted) – something*

many would agree is the height of absurdity for an enter-
prise that entertains peoples by locking them in a room for
an hour and giving them loads of puzzles that they must
solve before being let back out! On top of this, because
B.R.A.I.N is not only a place where people go to escape
but also to enjoy themselves – what with all the exhibi-
tions (not to mention the parties, etc.) organized around
it – B.R.A.I.N wants to live by letting you experience all
these extraordinary adventures. Which is why we're giving
you a chance to support us through this fundraiser.

The story being told on the game platform exudes authenticity. Eve-ryone understands that the people involved, driven by their passion for escape games, find themselves in a delicate situation; they are on a journey, going through a difficult initiation phase, and it is this that mobilizes their target audience around the cause.

Online challenges and fundraisers are just two examples of the things that start-up founders can use to drive engagement around their brand and generate interaction between people who will then sustain a community. The Canadian company Loop exemplifies how the defence of a cause (and the recruitment of volunteers) sparks participation in a challenge that mobilizes a community. David Côté, who was already responsible for several entrepreneur-ial successes in Montreal (Crudessence and Rise Kombucha), went even further with Loop,[22] a circular economy project born out of a group of dreamers gathered around a cause, a rescue mission com-ing to the aid of people unloved by the food industry. While tools are available to create links between consumers, what truly builds interactions between consumers is a mission that is far greater than both the company and its founder.

The expansion of the Internet and of social networks over the past 20 years has led to a marked increase in forms of interac-tion. Yet there was nothing automatic about this happening. Many brand communities have also been created and developed around physical interactions and gatherings. Above all, on- and offline interactions are being increasingly combined thanks to the online sharing (and subsequent discussion and re-posting) of photos and videos taken during physical events.

NOTES

1. Stephen Brown. "Marketing for Muggles: The Harry Potter way to higher profits." *Business Horizons* 45(1), 6–14, 2002.

2. Alex Wipperfürth, "Brand hijack." In *Marketing Without Marketing*, New York, NY: Portfolio, 2005.

3. https://www.lefigaro.fr/actualite-france/2008/07/16/01016-20080716 ARTFIG00321-roselyne-bachelot-conseille-le-boycott-du-red-bull-.php

4. https://www.lemonde.fr/sante/article/2012/06/25/vodka-red-bull-le-cocktailexplosif_1723633_1651302.html

5. Alex Wipperfürth, "Brand hijack." In *Marketing Without Marketing*, New York, NY: Portfolio, 2005.

6. https://www.redbull.com/us-en/best-of-red-bull-flugtag-2019-01-07

7. https://www.redbull.com/fr-fr/tags/soap-box-race

8. https://asia.nikkei.com/Politics/Turbulent-Thailand/Red-Bull-boycott-From-Thai-pride-to-symbol-of-inequality

9. Victor Turner, *The Ritual Process: Structure and Antistructure*, Chicago, IL: Aldine, 1969.

10. Luc Boltanski & Eve Chiappello, *The New Spirit of Capitalism*, trans. Gregory Elliott, London: Verso, 2005.

11. https://leprescripteur.prescriptionlab.com/justine-hutteau-ma-tumeur-a-la-poitrine-a-ete-un-declic/

12. https://www.huffpost.com/archive/qc/entry/poches-fils-ouverture-premiere-boutique_qc_5e690852c5b68d61645ea8bc

13. https://www.wsj.com/articles/SB848614878165890000

14. https://www.wsj.com/articles/SB848614878165890000

15. https://www.wsj.com/articles/SB848614878165890000

16. https://twitter.com/lasvegasstrong?

17. https://www.britannica.com/story/what-is-the-significance-of-the-oscarssowhite-hashtag

18. https://shortyawards.com/7th/putacanonit

19. https://www.tiktok.com/tag/laredoutechallenge

20. https://lareclame.fr/fredfaridgroup-bilan-laredoute-challenge-tiktok-238579

21. https://www.brain-escapegame-caen.fr/

22. https://loopmission.com/pages/about

5

DEVELOPING RITUALS

Every social relationship needs rites if it is going to develop and endure. Every social group needs rites to affirm and reaffirm its existence plus the fact that it has members. No community of consumers can much less endure in the absence of rites. Given the importance that entrepreneurs attribute to communities nowadays, rituals can no longer be considered as mere historic relics limited to religious contexts. Quite the contrary, they have become an integral part of contemporary entrepreneurialism. New rituals must be created to accompany the invention of any new product or service offer, brand or experience. Indeed, this specific type of inventiveness has become an essential activity for managers seeking to consolidate their brand consumers' sense of belonging to a community.

This 'revenge of rituals', as anthropologists have called it, is a recent phenomenon and/or, at the very least, a symptom of humankind's transition into the third millennium. Whereas the decades following the cultural watershed that was 1968 witnessed the elimination of many of the rituals that had previously cluttered people's lives – including but not limited to religious ceremonies – the past 20 years have seen a return in force both of certain rituals that had been partially abandoned previously, as well as the recurring creation of new ceremonies. Examples include the renewed popularity of baby showers, a largely female event celebrating a pregnancy and/or imminent arrival of a baby. There is little doubt that the great uncertainty plaguing the current era played a big role in this revenge. Whereas people tended during the post-1968 years to view rituals as an obstacle to personal freedom, the greater emphasis nowadays is on how they help to build connectivity, enabling consociality without creating any real sense of obligation.

Inventing new rituals is not easy, however, nor is it something that can be learned on some business or engineering course (indeed, the better option may be studying design or religion). The problem is that a very large number of rituals must be created before finding one that is capable of breaking through and being adopted by consumers to the point of structuring their lives and community relations. This might involve a simple gesture like a pupil 'turning, tasting and dipping' an Oreo cookie (in milk) – or else a more consequential ceremony like Denmark's early celebration of Christmas on the first Friday of November, when a traditional carriage arrives in the streets of Copenhagen at 9.59 p.m. precisely carrying a batch of Tuborg's Julebryg beer, specially brewed for the occasion. In both cases, consumers perform a ritual together with other people: classmates for the Oreo cookie; friends and fellow beer drinkers for Tuborg. The ritual is neither a solitary nor a spontaneous activity.

The first section of this chapter explains how rituals have transcended the religious sphere to invade everyone's daily lives. The second articulates the difference between micro-rites and macro-rites. This is followed by a section highlighting one of the most powerful of all commercial macro-rites – namely, the brand party – with details being offered about how start-ups emanating from a variety of sectors have consolidated their respective communities by injecting rituals into their product or service offers. The chapter then concludes with a dive into the more 'retro' phenomenon of business founders' reappropriation and restoration of ancient rituals that had partially (or sometimes, totally) disappeared.

RITES: FROM THE SACRED TO THE PROFANE

Since Emile Durkheim, rites have been seen as a way in which social reality announces and consolidates its durability. The three functions performed by rites called 'religious' are belief affirmation, uncertainty reduction and societal integration. Nowadays, however, many would say that these very same aspects can also be found in the so-called secular or contemporary rites, reflecting postmodern society's sacred dimension.[1]

It is very possible that rites have indeed been freed from the religious contexts with which they used to be associated to become a general expression of society and culture. In this view, secular rites' functioning correlates to their social utility, that is, their execution is essential to a periodic reinvigoration of society's moral fibre. Their purpose therefore becomes to connect the present to the past and the individual to the community. They bind discontinuous elements together and plug holes. By adapting rules and roles within the framework of the order they express, they bolster social integration, becoming both a process that exalts collective meaning (integration) and a device for regulating social relations (order).

Rites or rituals are sets of formalized and expressive acts imbued with a symbolic dimension. They also constitute an ordered sequencing of behaviour, one that is more rigid and predictable than ordinary actions are. Every rite has its recurring temporalities; models (the ones recited throughout history); and spatial partitions (the stages on which it performs). The whole process overflows with significance yet remains barely if at all aware of the theatrical roles it is being asked to perform; the values and purposes that it is conveying; the real and symbolic means at its disposal; or the coded systems that it uses to communicate. A rite's strength is partly measured by the emotions it arouses, ones sustained by the attention they require from all the masters of ceremony, audiences and participants communicating in this way. In turn, these emotions are affected by the metaphors that the rite is itself conveying – metaphors whose psychic resonance is all the greater because they are themselves embedded in living situations.

Longitudinal analysis separates rites into four main categories that redefine and specify the idea that a difference exists between general and singular occurrences:

- rites of passage or initiatory rites (e.g. graduation ceremonies at top universities);

- calendar rites or commemorative rites (like the 16 December 'ugly' Christmas sweater day);

- cyclical rites (like the Friday night parties); and

- occasional rites (like signing the cast on a person's broken arm).

Grosso mode, two types of rites can be distinguished:

- *Interactive micro-rites*. These are easy-to-manage systems facilitating human contact (and not meaningless vestiges of ancient politeness). They respond to specific needs arising in everyday situations, like the psychological need for self-protection or the communicational need for easier social contact.

- *Integrative macro-rites*. These are the somewhat bulkier systems that tend to be used to consolidate group membership. They are rooted in ideas like gift-giving, spending and sacrifice, always in relation to something deemed sacred and intended to re-bind (as per 're-ligion', from the Latin *re-ligare*) communities while staving off utilitarianism.

The important thing here is to delineate the clear distinction that exists between rituals (whether macro or micro) and ritualized behaviours, that is, minor and/or routine acts exemplified, for instance, by beauty care. It happens too often that entrepreneurs who have discovered how useful rites can be within a commercial approach – yet remain in hock to an individualistic mindset – view rites solely as routines performed by solitary individuals, despite the fact that rites' main power actually resides in their social dimension. Similarly, jamming a lemon slice into the neck of a Corona beer bottle – something that importers of this Mexican beverage often recommend – involves individual but not collective behaviour. Of course, it is an action that can also be shared: either directly when drinking with friends; or virtually by posting photos online. It remains that this was initially a ritualized behaviour, if only because it required no interaction with other consumers. Ritualized behaviours may have notoriously significant commercial impacts but it would be a real mistake to affirm that the power of consumption-related rites is limited to such behaviours alone.

COMMERCIAL MICRO-RITES AND MACRO-RITES

Above and beyond the aforementioned ritualized behaviours, consumption (and consumer) spheres are very aware of how important
both lesser micro-rites and greater macro-rites can be. Some rituals
emerge spontaneously from consumer practice whereas others are
created by an organization pursuing strategic intent before they
were ultimately adopted by consumers.

The Jeep Wave micro-rite story evoked in Chapter 1 typifies
a commercial rite's spontaneous emergence. Whenever one Jeep
Wrangler driver see another, they will always salute. This is because
Jeep Wrangler drivers share more than a mutual appreciation of
the vehicle – they feel part of a community. Note it was the Jeep
that won World War II, or to be more precise, that transported
generals and officers on their way to victory. It has been a mainstay
on every battlefield since then and often plays a leading role in war-
related films and TV series, all of which quickly helped propel it to
the forefront of popular culture. As a result, Jeep drivers in general
and Wrangler drivers in particular have an unstated rule that when
they cross paths, they should salute each other much as U.S. Army
officers did during World War II – a gesture that veterans continued
after returning home. There is even a name for Jeep owners' small
innocuous gesture of recognition – the Jeep Wave.[2] The end result
is that the Jeep brand has become very community-based, similar
to Harley-Davidson for motorcycles. The ritual makes people feel
they belong to a community while specifying everyone's rank within it. Moreover, not only do Jeep owners have to salute when they
see one another around town but there is also the expectation that
the interaction be initiated by the person driving the latest and/or
less powerful model – at which point, the other driver is expected
to salute in return.

Black Friday is a commercial macro-rite model invented by
American interests in the 1970s and promoted widely in the hope
that customers would buy in. The deeper origins of this event are
lost in the annals of US history, although some believe it harks back
to Black Thursday in 1929 when stock prices collapsed, kicking off
the Great Depression of the 1930s. As the fourth Friday in November (the one following Thanksgiving) approaches, mailboxes

overflow with tempting commercial offers allowing consumers to either buy their loved ones' Christmas gifts early or simply get ridiculously cheap deals. The recurring temporalities and spatial partitions associated with this macro-rite will then become visible in stores all across North America:

- 5 p.m. Consumers queue outside until the store opens, even in freezing weather. The excitement is palpable.

- 9 p.m. A sales assistant opens the doors. The crowd loses itself inside the store, with people jostling one another and stumbling all over the place. Everyone hopes to achieve outcomes as good as the ones that were promised. The crowd loses itself in a purchasing frenzy, coveting objects because it sees everyone else thinking and doing the same. Within this mass of bodies, consumers forget the social norms that usually govern public behaviour, engaging in a rivalrous relationship with one another. Lust creates enemies. People deploy different strategies in the hope of appropriating the objects they desire – strategies that can cause harm to fellow shoppers, now seen as rivals.

Astonishingly, the violence witnessed across the United States on Black Friday seems to be legitimized. People surviving these scrums and coming out with the item(s) they desired are euphoric and feel that they stand out from the masses. Brandishing their trophies, they feel special. Note that Black Friday has been similarly structured in France for many years, albeit with one cultural adaptation – namely that the doors open at midnight and not at 9 p.m.

Another macro-rite story that everyone in France knows also bears witness to the power of rites. Every third Thursday in November, the famous cry goes out all across the country that 'the *Beaujolais nouveau* has arrived'. The origins of this macro-rite go back to World War II, which devastated the Beaujolais region to such an extent that it was no longer able to export the local wine (which was also becoming less popular). It was at this point that a wine merchant called Georges Duboeuf created a tradition from scratch, one revolving around wines in their *primeur*, pre-bottled state. Duboeuf's idea was to develop an economic model in which large quantities of inexpensive wine would hit the market at a time of the year when there is always a seasonal shortage. The French government made things easier for him by accrediting a new *Beaujolais nouveau* appellation in 1951 – since which time the only new vintages licensed for sale before December 15 have been barely macerated wines of this type. In the early years, the event was always set for November 15 so that winegrowers could harmonize their sales projections, with the date moving to the third Thursday in November in 1985. Scheduling an annual event has allowed merchants to build massive marketing campaigns around the first bottles being uncorked, and raising consumer expectations in this way. Officially, the first bottles can only be opened after midnight, once Wednesday has become Thursday. By evening, huge crowds of French fans are gathering in the country's bars, restaurants and wine shops to taste and comment on the year's *Beaujolais nouveau*. Refusing to join the ritual is very hard to do if a person does not want to exude the impression of being socially marginalized. Consumption rituals' strength resides in the way that some people force others to join in.

The *Beaujolais nouveau* example is interesting because it elucidates a common confusion about company-related rites. The rites associated with the wine are unique first and foremost because they are consumer rites that transform into corporate rites whenever a business uses them to advance social cohesion in the workplace. All companies create rites to engage staff members. Start-up founders can always do the same but corporate rites (whether micro or macro) are generally not meant to consolidate a consumer community around a brand. Instead, their vocation is to focus on internal targets, starting with employees.

BRANDFESTS: A CONTEMPORARY MACRO-RITE BOTH ONLINE AND OFFLINE

Brandfests like the World Nutella Day[3] are one of today world's most powerful consumer macro-rites. Created in 1964, Nutella generates extraordinary enthusiasm – as evidenced by the emergence of bona fide *nutellari* fan clubs, Nutella Parties and other group events celebrating this much-loved hazelnut spread. Such events are particularly widespread in Italy where they are organized by groups of all ages in formats ranging from village or neighbourhood festivals to school parties. Nutella has become such a phenomenon that books have been published discussing its history, secret recipe or diehard fan base, the best way of enjoying it, etc. There are cooking books offering nothing other than Nutella-based recipes. One of the leading showcases for this huge success story is the Internet. Typing Nutella on Google triggers an avalanche of results with a Facebook page featuring tens of millions of fans. In 2007, a young American living in Italy (Sara Rosso[4]) decided that every February 5 should henceforth be called World Nutella Day, with fans being invited to share their favourite recipes and commune with one another by promising to eat spoonfuls of Nutella ('We have a dream. And a spoon – Nutella lovers unite just for one day – Nutella Day'). Rosso chose that particular date because of its proximity to Candlemas, a Christian holiday when people traditionally eat pancakes, which they were now being encouraged to enjoy with Nutella. The idea was to time the event after the New Year and also before Lent so that it would not happen at a time of the year when some people are depriving themselves of chocolates and other sweets.

Rosso's organizational work started with the launch of a NutellaDay.com website featuring more than 700 links to recipes uploaded by bloggers worldwide. An unofficial Nutella guide has even been published telling the story of how Pietro Ferrero invented his hazelnut spread in 1947; listing the best recipes using this famous Italian product; and advising people 'How to Host a World Nutella Day Party at Home'. The site encourages brand enthusiasts to share their own Nutella-related stories in the form of texts, photos, videos or poems. There is also a regularly scheduled online slot devoted to Nutella, with people posting material to dedicated addresses on Facebook, Instagram, Pinterest, Twitter and YouTube. Many restaurants also take part in the fun by preparing special Nutella Day menus so that everyone can participate in the macro-rite.

Nutella's brandfest is not an isolated case. May 4, named Star Wars Day,[5] sees fans celebrating a different kind of saga but one that is just as well-known. This increasingly global initiative stems from a simple play on words between the film franchise's famous catchphrase 'May the Force be with you' – a leitmotif for heroes like Luke Skywalker, Anakin Skywalker and Obi-Wan Kenobi fighting the forces of evil – and the phonetically similar phrase 'May the fourth be with you', identifying a specific date. Canada's Toronto Underground Cinema organized the first Star Wars Day party in 2011 based on this pun. Activities included a costume contest, a quiz about the original trilogy films and a presentation of the best tribute films, parodies and remixes found online. The geek culture that dominated the Internet in 2011 helped the day to quickly become famous and globalize. May 4 is so important to Star Wars fans that they are prepared, if need be, to take the day off work to celebrate it properly. Of course, part of the event is wearing costumes, meeting other fans and even producing shows. The end result is that since 2013, May 4 has been celebrated worldwide as the official *Star Wars Day*.

It would be wrong to deduce from this that brandfests and other macro-rituals of this kind are solely the prerogative of big brands (like Star Wars) enjoying huge budgets. Take the example of the 'Garden Pâté'[6] that France's Hénaff brand organizes every year at Pouldreuzic in Brittany, an event that starts with a simple invitation extended via various social networks (but above all on a bespoke Garden Pâté Facebook page):

> *We have a date for the traditional Garden Pâté! It's Sunday, August 27, starting at noon on the Hénaff Museum front lawn. All Hénaff fans are welcome to this giant gathering. As always, bring your hampers and we'll take it from there! Come one come all, join us in enjoying Breton's famous sunshine;) And don't forget our GPS coordinates: 47°57'15.41"N and 04°22'15.07" With love, Team Hénaff.*

The meeting usually attracts around 3,000 diehard brand fans, picnicking on the grass in front of the La Maison du Pâté Hénaff museum with baskets full of blue boxes of pâté, cold cuts and sausages. The brand organizes funfair activities. Every year it chooses a specific theme, one recent example being outer space, with some guests disguising themselves as Hénaff astronauts or wearing

Breton-like hair coifs, including the little blue boxes. The brandfest always ends with a group photo, taken by a drone. A three-minute video clip is then posted on YouTube to publicize the ritual's power.

START-UPS AND THE CREATION OF RITES

A start-up brand has every interest in creating rituals and getting consumers to adopt them. This strengthens people's ties to the brand community and/or movement that is being initiated, while potentially increasing consumption volumes as well. There are no rules for designing a brand ritual or rite, however, despite the growing frequency of online Q&A and/or advice. Otherwise, inspiration can also be drawn from the success that entrepreneurs and/or the advocates of a cause have had with their own creations, which can then be adapted to the new project.

The SoulCycle Micro-rite: The Collective Blowing Out of Candles

SoulCycle studios always start their cycling sessions in the same way with a lemon-scented candle lit in the reception area. Participants then go to the warm-up room, which will also be lit by similarly scented candles. Once everyone has returned to the cycling room, the lighting flickers between darkness (so people can centre themselves) and light (a time for communal sharing). The micro-rite comes at the end of the workout when the coach asks three or four participants to join in blowing out the candles, thereby signalling a symbolic end to the session – following which participants can again talk, congratulate and/or embrace one another.

The Tough Mudder Micro-rite: Swapping Photos of People Wearing a Brand Headband

As noted in Chapter 1, Tough Mudder race participants are always very proud when they complete the ordeal. They are ritually handed a cold beer when they get to the finish line, plus an orange headband with the Tough Mudder logo. The banner symbolizes all the work that everyone had to do in preparing for a race run as a team, only completing it after overcoming 25 obstacles (and tons of mud). Tough Mudder headbands are tantamount to a kind of reward. Some participants own two or three of them – rising to as many as ten if they have done the race repeatedly. It is at this level that rituals and social networks come into play. Having noted customers' enthusiasm for taking pictures of themselves wearing their headbands, Will Dean, Tough Mudder's founder, initiated a Facebook ritual called Headband Monday. This consists of people uploading on this one day of the week photos or videos of themselves wearing the famous orange headband. There is nothing to be gained from this other than the pleasure of harvesting – just before the workweek begins – a few 'like' emojis and community member feedback. In the same vein but less delicately, Taco Bell is a fast-food chain whose popularity in the United States has been enhanced by certain customers' habit of exchanging photos or illustrations of their digestive experiences after a meal in one of the brand's restaurants. Social media helped to popularize this aspect of going to a Taco Bell, although the company (quite understandably) has never wanted to make an institutionalized ritual out of it.

Silent Night, a Silent Macro-rite

The Taylor University Trojans basketball team in Upland (IN, USA) performs a Silent Night ritual once a year. On the Friday before the December final exam period, fans are asked to remain silent until their team scores ten points – at which juncture, the arena explodes with joy and good humour. Screaming spectators might throw themselves at the players or wear some fairly off-the-wall costumes, ranging from the alien in Toy Story to Olaf from Frozen. This macro-ritual has been performed since 1997 (except for 2020, due to Covid-19).

The Teddy Bear Toss, a Charitable Macro-rite

This North American tradition dates back to the early 1990s. In the run-up to Christmas, fans bring teddy bears to an ice hockey game and throw them onto the rink when their team scores its first goal. The so-called 'Teddy bear toss' not only generates lovely images that everyone enjoys but has also spawned a whole new vocation, with players and volunteers alike collecting the toys and distributing them to various charities or hospitals, which make Christmas presents out of them for underprivileged locals. Fans of the Calgary Hitmen, a team in one of Canada's junior ice hockey leagues, set a record in their December 2015 match against the Swift Current Broncos when a torrent of 28,815 fluffy toys rained on the ice immediately after the Hitmen's first goal. Play was interrupted for the nearly 40 minutes it took to gather all the teddy bears. The interruption boded well for Calgary, however, which ended up winning 2–1.

Many other examples of rituals-related creativity in North American universities can be found in a beautiful book authored by Stan Beck and Jack Wilkinson, who have identified more than 100 micro-rites and macro-rites that some of world's most famous institutions of higher education have been using to create greater community cohesion.[7]

REWRITING RITUALS

Despite there being no rules prescribing how branded rituals are to be created, past examples offer some inspiration. One noteworthy case is the 'revival' of absinthe and the rituals associated with this drink. Absinthe has always been prepared and drunk in a very specific way. Indeed, the ritual is part of the product's charm and contributes to its popularity and unique position in the pantheon of alcoholic beverages. All true absinthes are at least slightly bitter, due in part to the traces of absinthine found in the final brew. This explains why the drink is usually served with sugar, which counterbalances the bitterness but also nurtures the herbal aromas and floral fragrances. The traditional French ritual begins with about 30 ml of absinthe being poured into a glass, ideally a bespoke one. A sugar cube is placed on a perforated flat spoon resting on the glass's edge. Ice water is then poured very slowly over the sugar, which gradually dissolves drip by drip. This sends ripples through the green liquid below, which then turns cloudy with a milky opaqueness. The usual ratio is usually three to four doses of water for every dose of 136 proof absinthe. The hardcore absinthe drinkers of yesteryear would pour water very gently and admire the milky tracks that each drop left in the 'wormwood'. Observing changes in the colour of the liquid became key to the ritual's pleasure.

The fascination with absinthe has always been closely related to the ritual associated with it. No other beverage requires such a meticulous ceremony, one enshrining the whole experience in a drug-like mystique. All historical accounts attest to the universal nature of this way of imbibing absinthe, with even the most destitute of workers – drinking in the most down-in-the-mouth bar or café – taking the time to brew the concoction correctly. Of course, the performance of the ritual could also vary, including with the use of sugar alternatives like gum syrup (*absinthe gommée*) or sweet anise liqueur ('aniseed absinthe'). Occasionally, the concoction would even be diluted with a weaker alcohol like white wine ('midnight absinthe') or cognac (for painter Toulouse Lautrec's favourite drink, called the 'earthquake'). These daring consumption techniques would heighten people's interest – but also, just as often, be met with criticism.

Due to one of the molecules found in a wormwood plant (thujone), absinthe has been accused of causing serious brain damage, associated with the kinds of hallucinations that Émile Zola described in his masterpiece, *L'Assommoir*. Many countries, including France in 1915, banned its consumption in the early twentieth century, explaining absinthe's long-term disappearance from store shelves – but not from the collective imagination. It took until 1998 for a British entrepreneur, Georges Rowley,[8] to 'relaunch' the drink with a product he called Hill's Absinth – which was actually a degraded version of the original variety, featuring a thujone content of less than 35 mg/l as prescribed under new European legislation. Rowley had discovered the flavour during a trip to Prague shortly after the Fall of the Berlin Wall. He combined this rebirth with a ritual that was inauthentic (in the sense that it did not correspond to the original), but which would nevertheless come to be seen as a useful innovation inspired by the way Italian Sambuca and other drinks of its kind are often lit with a match before being consumed. One measure of wormwood is now poured into a glass, alongside a piece of absinthe-soaked sugar that is lit and left to burn until it foams and caramelizes. The spoon with the caramelized sugar is then immersed in wormwood, often creating a flame that is extinguished with a dose of ice water. This so-called 'Bohemian' ritual took little time to conquer London and ensure the success of Hill's Absinth. It is an inauthentic ritual that has become so popular that it appears in several films, including Moulin Rouge. Despite being a historical heresy that would have horrified any *Belle Époque* absinthe fan, it has helped today's consumers become fans of Hill's Absinth and guaranteed the brand's rapid success.

A surprising twist in this tale, once Rowley's success had been assured with Hill's Absinth and its Bohemian ritual, was the entrepreneur's attempt to 'revive' authentic French absinthe (along with its own traditional French ritual) by creating a brand called *La Fée* in partnership with the *Musée de l'Absinthe*, located at Auvers-sur-Oise just outside Paris. Rowley may have felt remorse for his role in transforming absinthe's original ritual – but generally speaking there is no real need for founders to be overconcerned with their ritual's authenticity. The authors of this book are aware of few if any rituals that have not been altered, developed or reoriented over many decades (and for some, centuries). What matters for founders is the ability to mobilize a simple ritual that consumers might then teach one another. This is what happened with the new Bohemian ritual since it has enabled confirmed absinthe drinkers to train novices – the end result being that a ritual rooted in an idea of mutual support would ultimately strengthen a whole community. Note that the same simplicity explains the similar success that the Corona beer ritual had in Europe. It suffices that a twist of lime be stuffed in the bottle neck and the ritual has been performed. Of course, it is not something Mexicans do when drinking Corona back home, that is, the ritual such as it is being performed in Europe is authentic but also adapted.

In short, start-up founders mobilize two main types of rituals: daily micro-rituals carried out in small groups; and macro-rituals celebrating a brand on special occasions. Rituals do not demand any particularly creative efforts. Quite the contrary, companies will often reproduce something that has been done before, or which is being done elsewhere and simply requires a little adaptation. The lucky ones tend to draw inspiration from the rituals that their own consumers have invented – as long as they are not too off-the-wall, like the ritual invented by fans of the 8.6 beer produced by Bavaria who every June 8 drink as much of this very strong alcoholic beverage as they possibly can. Simplicity is key. Communities do not adopt overly complicated rituals.

Lastly, it should be made clear that a ritual must not require extra meetings. One case in point is an energy savings consultancy that announced a ritual requiring employees to meet regularly two-by-two to discuss any successes they had had, challenges they had faced, etc. In actual fact there was nothing very ritualistic about these meetings, characterized as they were by the absence of any fixed scheduling, dedicated spaces or (and above all) particularly strong emotions. But they were meetings and therefore clogged up participants' workweek. This is very different from the kinds of rituals that people definitely do not want to miss because it would marginalize them from their family, group or community. Examples include family Christmas celebrations on December 25, refusing to sign a friend's cast (or vice versa) or denying a fellow Jeep driver the pleasure of returning their salute. Rituals are inseparable from the life of any human group – and therefore from the life of any brand community.

NOTES

1. Émile Durkheim, *The Elementary Forms of the Religious Life [1912]*, New York, NY: Macmillan, 1995.

2. https://jeeps.thefuntimesguide.com/jeep_wave/

3. https://www.nutella.com/us/en/world-nutella-day

4. https://www.youtube.com/watch?v=qpwWWGOVsHw

5. https://www.starwars.com/star-wars-day

6. www.henaff.com

7. Stan Beck & Jack Wilkinson, *College Sports Traditions: Picking Up Butch, Silent Night, and Hundreds of Others*, Plymouth: The Scarecrow Press, 2013.

8. https://www.diffordsguide.com/producer/1099/la-fee/history

6

ADDING LINKING VALUE TO
THE VALUE PROPOSITION

Start-up founders often think up ideas and develop them by setting their sights on what future customers are supposed to be offered. Even if a community and volunteers are present during this early phase, founders still run a risk of stumbling over a number of economic hurdles just as they are beginning to put together a business model, hence define a value proposition. The normal reflex is to conceptualize an average customer profile and reason in terms of the best way of serving and satisfying him or her. But this means constructing a project around an abstraction, making it easier to lose sight of the wider community – even though that is precisely where the focus should be. A company's product or service offer must enable community members to meet and enjoy the time they spend together. A community is no good if everyone's acts of consumption are done in isolation.

The most recognizable situation is one where start-up founders who are in the process of developing their business projects or models view communities as little more than simple tools to be instrumentalized via a marketing approach. It is a mindset where business founders ignore the possibilities they have of using a product or service offer to create a community, focusing instead on communications alone. Clearly the better option is to make the community – and the linking value that comes with it – central to the product or service offer, which should be designed to prioritize teams, groups and communities rather than isolated consumers. Business offers that revolve around a collective online or offline experience help create a potentially permanent connection between everyone sharing in an emotion, who will then go on to fortify the community through the interactions they have during and (especially) after the experience. Business founders add value to their proposition if they conceptualize things first and foremost in terms of what is being offered to teams of individuals and not to single individuals. Some may object that this kind of value assessment carries little weight in potential customers' decision whether or not to purchase whatever it is that the start-up is offering. The following section tries to prove that this critique is unjustified by offering examples of start-ups whose success has been rooted in a team focus – especially given the great value that the postmodern world places on connectivity (all the more so in an era marked by Covid-19-related lockdowns).

The chapter's first section shows how changes in people's daily lives cause them to renew their search for connectivity, hence to develop a greater appreciation of a product or service offer's linking value. The second section explains how this connection is co-produced by a start-up in conjunction with its consumers and not all by itself. The third second details the fantastic success that one start-up has had in altering a specific individual practice, transforming it into a collective action and co-producing linking value in this way. The chapter concludes with a counterexample highlighting the cost for new brands of ignoring linking value.

FROM SOCIAL CONNECTIVITY TO LINKING VALUE

As demonstrated above, the postmodern world has replaced social reality with consociality. Individuals nowadays form networks defined by relational structures that are more fluid and unstable than the ones traditional communities used to experience. What connects individuals to a stable community today counts less than what connects them to one another. The specific community to which someone belongs matters less since it is individuals themselves who increasingly constitute the focal point (or at the very least, the point of departure) for social connectivity. What this means is that social connections have weakened, with postmodern society reacting to this state of affairs by engaging in a whole host of initiatives based on a variety of methods, all of which seek to rebuild personal connections. Examples include neighbours days; street festivals; communal dining; and, of course, a whole host of online platforms and apps. Rather than highlighting the overarching nature of these connections, it is their emergent quality that should be emphasized. By so doing, the analysis transcends the idea of social connectivity to develop a construct of consociality, which is a more accurate way of depicting these intra-personal configurations. Consociality[1] can be understood as the action by means of which individuals come into contact (and maintain contact) with one another, be it online or offline. People's constant rearrangement of their spheres of sociality lends itself to an understanding that is more fluid, but also more unstable, than the social reality which communities experienced in the past.

This transition offers companies a number of opportunities. Where they used to destroy social connectivity by offering products or services that had the effect of freeing consumers from social constraints, their role today is to help develop the kinds of consocial connections that correspond more closely to current yearnings. That being the case, the connectivity that a company helps to foster becomes more important to consumers than the items it offers, that is, goods end up being purchased more because they enhance sociality than for their actual functionality. The linking value associated with a product, service or brand can then be defined as the value that it provides in helping to build or strengthen individual connections, a linking value akin to an unconventional use value, with the product being useful precisely because it supports connectivity.[2] This understanding is rarely part of customary use value analysis, which tends to only recognize an item's immediate use – a conception ignoring the fact that products and services can bolster the ties that people build with one another, a utility that is sufficiently different from other kinds of use value to merit its own discussion.

The proposition here is that start-ups' product and service offer should be analyzed in light of their linking value, intimating a new focus on how a company can help build, develop and maintain connections between consumers. It is a much broader vision of the purpose of a company than one where it is reduced to an entity whose only goal is to deliver given outputs to isolated customers. This not entirely unprecedented conception can be equated – as Michèle de la Pradelle[3] did in her study of local markets in France's Provence region – to a resurgent form of pre-modern trade. What is new in the life of each individual is the intensity and importance of intra-consumer connections that are best analyzed as being 'socio-commercial' in nature. Postmodern society's search for connectivity is something that companies are increasingly incorporating into their thinking. People can weave entire networks of sociality based solely on commercial offers that include some kind of linking value and which mitigate any commercial dimensions they may have developed in this way – justifying in turn a new focus on the marketing of connectivity.

The Covid-19 crisis has disrupted this stasis while demonstrating how important these consociality bonds are to daily life. Lockdowns, when people are supposed to wear masks and respect social distancing, have created a new, contactless kind of interaction, one that impedes the creation and maintenance of social connections, if only because it undermines the traditional reciprocity (give–receive–give) principle that has been the anthropological basis of human interaction for time immemorial. Of course, this interaction obstacle has crept into the commercial domain, affecting for instance payments but also communications with retailers (all the more so because many products are themselves considered suspicious nowadays). Yet as noted below, lockdowns have also been a reminder that humans are social animals with a need to feel, touch and kiss. For many people, it was during lockdown that they actually realized how much they need other people and human contact.

The search for individual freedom – a significant contributory factor in the weakening of social bonds – is at odds with a public health reality that forces people to reduce the number and quality of their contacts. Many find this unbearable, especially when it is portrayed as obligation. Paradoxically, it is in the name of individual freedom that postmodern society often claims a right to connectivity – often translating into the core demand that shops must remain open, in large part because if businesses are closed, there will be fewer opportunities for connections. It is not only because postmodern individuals need to get supplies that many are demanding that shops remain open. It is also because they want to preserve the socio-commercial connections that have structured their lives up until now. In short, the health crisis has shone a light on the immense value that people associate with shops (or indeed, bars and restaurants). The question then becomes where this linking value comes from – and the respective roles that companies and consumers play in its production.

LINKING VALUE: A CONSUMER CO-PRODUCTION

Companies do not produce linking value but they can encourage it by creating a context conducive to its development. The key element here is making it easier for consumers to help one another – something, it is worth noting, quite different from the facilitation of sharing, a false conflation often found in economic analysis. Social sciences tend to envision three main types of altruistic behaviour: mutual assistance/helping; sharing and comforting. One example is if someone's friend loses their wallet, a person can either help them look for it (helping); give money to tide them over (sharing) or manifest compassion (comforting). Mutual assistance/helping means understanding another person's needs and addressing them through one's own actions. Sharing means understanding their desire and resolving it in a material way. Comforting means being aware of their negative emotional state and offering the appropriate support. Clearly, sharing incorporates a sense of helping, like when children share their food (or adults their expertise) with other people. The behaviours are close and can both be classified as altruistic – but they are different. It is possible to help a person without sharing, for example, one's tangible goods with them. Many of the situations where consumers help one another involve more of a phenomenon of giving (of time, of oneself) than of sharing. The fact of receiving then generates the desire to give something back in return. It is a fundamental social phenomenon in all societies. Indeed, society might not be able to exist without it.

The Tough Mudder obstacle course case study discussed in Chapter 1 is instructive in this regard. The company's website notes, for instance, how difficult it is to complete the challenge by oneself, emphasizing the possibility of doing the event in teams whose members help one another. This starts with a formal pledge before the race 'I put teamwork and comradery before my course time .... I help my fellow Mudders complete the course'. The success of this kind of brand experience is actually predicated on people helping each another – or as one participant testified[4]:

> The team keeps you involved. You always wonder if every-
> one is still there. We join hands, we help each other over-
> come obstacles and if one person is slower than everyone
> else, we wait for them.

Indeed, one of the best things about the experience is feeling part of a team: 'For four hours you're getting help from people you don't know. The whole race feels like a moment of altruism'. In other words, Tough Mudder relies as a company on people's desire to help one another within a community context – an experience it sells for €150 a head.

In a similar vein, it is not really possible to take part in an escape room session all by oneself. Organizers of this category of entertainment tend to think that the ideal number of participants is between four and five. As a reminder, the activity involves people being locked together in a room symbolizing an enclosed place (castle, pirate ship, Egyptian pyramid, prison, distant planet, etc.) and having a limited amount of time to jointly investigate and solve the riddles that will allow them to escape. Teams formed in this way will possess enough hands to search the escape room, plus enough joint intelligence to solve any riddles. Above all, participants are not supposed to unlock secrets all by themselves but instead communicate with one another so that everyone can escape together – and by so doing, turn the prisoners dilemma on its head.[5]

Mutual assistance between consumers produces value for participants but also – and above all – for the company, transforming the value generated around its brand into an exchange value from which it also benefits. The Tough Mudder business model that Will Dean invented has been doubly successful: the company spends nothing on generating a surplus value from which its customers derive a great deal of satisfaction; and it can charge more for its obstacles courses than competitors can. The entire business model revolves around the idea of consumers helping one another. From escape rooms to CrossFit rooms to online games like the World of Warcraft, today there is a growing list of brands taking advantage of (and capitalizing on) consumers' mutual assistance.

Nowadays, capturing the value that mutual assistance generates no longer depends on the offer being made to an isolated consumer (the central figure in traditional marketing) but on the organization of an experience that consumers enjoy together, thanks to the brand. Most importantly, the brand must be designed from the very outset around this helping construct – as exemplified by the many product and service offers that both feature strong linking value and create networks sustaining people's feelings of togetherness and comradery. In situations of this kind, consumers are encouraged to be thankful to one another, to recognize everyone's set of skills hence generate mutual recognition. Someone playing World of Warcraft online will benefit from the linking value generated through their participation in a 'guild'. Indeed, this must happen for them to have any hope of being able to progress through the game's different stages. Of course, there is also a price to pay for the experience, namely the subscription to Blizzard Entertainment, which owns the World of Warcraft brand.

REASONS FOR DOING TOGETHER WITH OTHERS THINGS THAT A PERSON CAN DO BY THEMSELF

One erroneous idea impeding the development of product or service offers that incorporate linking value is the notion that certain offers are individual in nature; that others are fundamentally collective and that nothing can be done to change this. The SoulCycle case shows that start-up founders are capable, if they so desire, of reinventing heretofore solitary practices and turning them into core components of a new offer featuring a high linking value. Indeed, this is what the company's designers – Ruth Zukerman, Elizabeth Cutler and Julie Rice – did when they re-imagined exercise bikes as tools to be used for collective practice instead of in individual isolation.

In the early 2000s, Ruth Zukerman was teaching aerobics at the Reebok Sports Club on New York City's Upper West Side.[6] Whenever she was off work, she would attend a work colleague's cycling classes. These were held in a space that can only be described as cossetted, something she found quasi-therapeutic. Given her passion for cycling, she decided to teach this activity herself but to add the personal touch of offering students an immersive experience replete with contemporary music punctuated by powerful lyrics. She also decided that she should talk to students as if she were a personal development coach. The sum total of these moves enhanced her courses' popularity and quickly led to their being sold out. Then in 2006, Zukerman brought two of her former students into the business: Elizabeth Cutler (formerly a real estate agent) and Julie Rice (who had been working as a talent manager in the entertainment industry). Rice and Cutler got along famously and in the course of their discussions came up with the idea of building a bespoken cycling centre, convincing Zukerman to join them in this enterprise.

The simple idea here was to transform how stationary cycling is practiced, changing it from a painful obligation into a pleasurable experience that would transform participants both internally and externally. The vision of the three entrepreneurs – making social connectivity and meaningfulness the core values in a business applying the Zukerman method – culminated in the birth of Soul-Cycle, a company and a brand whose name conveys its sense of self. SoulCycle quickly became a hit in New York City, with all of its trendier neighbourhoods – ranging from Greenwich Village to Union Square and Tribeca – all wanting their own SoulCycle club. David Beckham swears by this brand, as do Max Greenfield (from the New Girl series), Katie Holmes, Bradley Cooper, Katy Perry and other celebrities. Indeed, today this phenomenon stretches far past the confines of New York. The Big Apple hosted SoulCycle's first 31 indoor bicycle studio in 2006. By 2021, the company was running 95 studios in all major North American cities (including Chicago, Dallas, Austin, Houston and Toronto) and had expanded to Europe, starting in London.

SoulCycle represents itself as a renewal of stationary cycling, albeit in spaces featuring anywhere between 30 and 50 bicycles.

The basic idea is for people to get active in a dark space lit by only a few candles and with loud rhythmic music blasting in the background. Sessions last for 45 minutes and include exercises building up participants' upper bodies (push-ups using bicycle handlebars; obliques and biceps work using dumbbells, etc.). Coaches are always onsite to motivate the troops. Lights are dimmed, music volumes are turned up, shoes are clipped into the pedals and everyone is off and running for 45 minutes of SoulCycling while being hypnotized by the voice of the coach telling everyone 'Close your eyes, stop thinking, let's go!'

A number of factors explain the success of this North American venture: the studios' arty décor and minimalist design; the flashy yellow colours everywhere; the excitement of the experience itself; without forgetting its fantastic branding. Above all, however, there is the connection with other people, the fact that everyone is pedalling together. As SoulCycle's founders like to say,

> At SoulCycle we believe that fitness can be joyful. We climb, we jog, we sprint, we dance, we set our intention, and we break through boundaries. The best part? We do it together, as a community.[7]

SoulCycle offers the comforting warmth of a community that creates collective emotions/hallucinations. In this offering, coaches play a crucial role by producing linking value and developing a fan community. Attendance at a given session depends on the charisma of the coach, who is therefore incentivized to give their all each to every time. Coaches are all former athletes, dancers, actors and indeed ex-customers. Plus they are full-time employees whose presence is intended to motivate participants throughout the collective experience. At the end of the session, once everyone has warmed down, the coach is waiting as they leave the room, congratulating each participant and often hugging them. In the words of a customer[8]:

> Usually at the beginning of class the instructor encourages you to introduce yourself to the people around you. This is your 'team'. Throughout class the instructor will encourage the group by saying 'let's go team', 'ride for the person next you', things of that nature. Also during the class

you are encouraged to ride to the beat of the music, when the room is all riding to the same beat and on the same cadence, you feel as though you are part of a team routine. It connects you to everyone in the studio. Sometime as part of the routine you clap with your hands or the instructor guides you to touch the handle bars of the rider to your left to encourage them to go faster. It creates a sense of cama-raderie and encouragement with complete strangers. (Kari)

One salient question is how this kind of offering – with the pro-found linking value it incorporates – could survive the Covid-19 crisis. One answer is that starting in June 2020, SoulCycle started holding scrupulously socially distanced outdoor sessions in tents. An example from New York City was the Hudson Yards neighbour-hood site. Everything there was different asides from the station-ary cycles, first and foremost because there was neither music nor was the space darkened. The challenge for SoulCycle was therefore whether its magic would still work in this new configuration, one where session participants were more isolated because they were more physically distant and because each had headphones on. As described again by Kari:

[A] great song began piping in through my headphone and I could hear the instructors voice in my ear. Her voice on top of the beat of the music, she said 'what's up Soul Cycle – how good does it feel to be back home'. 'Find the beat on your right foot'. With that, the entire tent of 80 peo-ple stood up and rode together perfectly to the music. It was a climactic experience. I closed my eyes and listened to the instruction coming through the headphones and felt like maybe this was even better than the original? ... We cheered to being back together. I didn't matter that we didn't know each other, we were all part of the Soul Cycle tribe and therefore we were family. I took selfies with riders next to me and posted them online to talk about my incred-ible experience, I saw a lot of other riders do the same.[9]

Both before and during the Covid-19 crisis, SoulCycle's offer-ing incorporated a strong linking value that helped it to build a brand community. One way of conceptualizing the strength of this offering involves the antistructure construct that was first theorized by English anthropologist Victor Turner.[10] In this view, daily life occurs within a structure, a world where everyone lives for themself, trying to achieve personal goals, experiencing limited social interaction and marking their difference with others by erecting behavioural, vestimentary and other barriers. Certain experiences become a conduit into the antistructure, an alternative sphere within which people help one another to achieve collective goals, entertain numerous positive interactions and in so doing erase the barriers that separate them. According to Turner, this world comprises a *communitas*, with people's experiences seeming all the more alternative to them precisely because they are ephemeral. This is what SoulCycle offers and it epitomizes people's search for a linking value within a product or service offer, to wit, the fact that this value induces the antistructure's alternative reality.

THE CONSEQUENCES OF NOT GENERATING ANY LINKING VALUE

Whereas SoulCycle attests to the power of incorporating linking value into a product or service offer as soon as a brand is launched, it is also worth discussing the deleterious effects that arise over the medium term when such value is absent (even if efforts have been made to create it).

Scion is a Japanese car brand that the Toyota automotive group started from scratch in 2003 – but which had completely vanished by the year 2016. The brand only operated in the North American markets, where it targeted a younger customer base that had not been particularly attracted by Toyota, which it perceived as making cars for old folks. Toyota wanted to appeal to young Millennials, a group that would soon represent 60 million North American motorists and therefore outweigh the legendary Baby Boom generation. The risk for Toyota was to lose traction with this new cohort.

Toyota launched its Scion sub-brand with two models derived from cars that were already sold in Japan but whose hubcaps, hi-fi systems, seats, headlights, etc., could be significantly customized.

The key concept in the new business model was vehicle customization accessories representing more than 20% of the total purchasing price. Scions were offered by Toyota dealers through bespoke Scion Customization Centers tasked with all the adaptation work that needed to be done. Initials sales were dazzling, exceeding the 2005 target of 100,000 units by 50%. The year 2006 was Scion's best year for US sales, reaching a whopping 173,034 units – nearly twice its target, all of which boded well for the new brand ... and made its ensuing collapse all the more hellish, with US sales volumes dropping by the year 2015 by a factor of three to 56,167 units. In its 13 years of existence, Scion has sold exactly 1,122,809 units – barely 10% of what the Toyota Group sells in a single year worldwide.[11]

Initially, Scion's marketing intentions seemed original and off-beat enough to be in sync with what Millennials want. Managers spoke of cutting-edge marketing techniques, Internet sales, viral marketing, guerrilla marketing, a Second Life presence, an unprecedented level of accessory customization, Dream Car contests, etc. The communications campaign's key phrase was 'Everybody is trying to be different', with the Scion being advertised as a vehicle whose advanced customization meant it could be configured to fit everyone's personal style. The campaign slogan was 'What Moves You'. Automotive sector experts would later explain that one of the reasons for the brand's death was Toyota's inability to go far enough with its customization promise and failure to keep fully abreast of technological advances. Scion's direct rivals – like the Mini (relaunched in 2001 by BMW) with its Mini Yours Customized programme – were quick to attack it on this point.

Another explanation for Scion's post-2007 failure has to do with customer expectations. Where all of Scion's competitors – led by the Mini – played the community card by giving prospective customers the option of joining an existing community as soon as they purchased their vehicle, Scion emphasized personalization and people's differences. Yet times had changed. The postmodern quest for community clearly accelerated over the course of the 2000s, in part due to the rise of Web 2.0. Toyota executives reacted too late. In August 2008, Scion launched a new campaign called 'United by Individuality' featuring a convoy of 300 Scion owners driving to Boulder City (NV, USA) to take part in a Scion United event, akin to a Mini United-style party, replete with concerts. Brand manager Dawn Ahmed explained that, 'Working with the community is one of the most important things a brand can do'.[12] The desert happening did not spark the expected mobilization, however, and in the end the Scion community existed solely as a figment of brand marketing specialists' imagination.

When the starting point for a value proposition is basically to highlight, as Scion did, an object's individuation potentialities, it becomes almost impossible (barring some accident of history) to foster a community, especially if the product or service offer does not include any linking value. The absence of a community will then weaken the brand, especially in an industry where competitors can count on their own loyal communities. Incorporating linking value into a company's product or service offer is therefore crucial for project founders seeking to build, develop and maintain a community. In turn, this intimates that offers of this kind – rooted in human contact rather than isolation – are a preferred vector for consumers' consociality, a precondition for any start-up wishing to capitalize upon a given community. A company's value proposition is the central element of its business model. Developed with an eye towards target customers' needs and expectations, it materializes in the new company's products, services and brand experiences while also expressing how consumers benefit from this offer (which needs to be differentiated from the competition). Where start-ups derive linking value directly from a community, they are doing more than simply dressing up a vague product or service offer. Nor is such value a merely complementary or marginal benefit. Instead, it necessarily becomes a key feature in the company's value proposition, if only because it represents consumers' primary motivations due to the fact that the products, services or experiences that the new brand offers is what allows them to create and maintain relationships with fellow consumers, experience shared emotions, feel they belong to a club and enjoy the comradery that goes with this.

Of course, a company's value proposition also has a more functional component. Even so, consumers will buy a brand's products and services less for their utilitarian attributes than for the links they create, however ephemeral these may be. Entrepreneurs must take a longer-term view of interaction-driven linking value.

This is very different from developing a start-up on the basis of an essentially functional value proposition – if only because it takes time for a community to appropriate their offering.

NOTES

1. Robert V. Kozinets, *Netnography: Redefined*, London: Sage, 2015.

2. Jacques Godbout & Alain Caillé, *World of the Gift*, Montréal: McGill-Queen's Press-MQUP, 1998.

3. Michelle de la Pradelle, *Market Day in Provence*, Chicago, IL: University of Chicago Press, 2006.

4. Bernard Cova & Eric Rémy, "Au coeur du phénomène collaboratif: l'entraide." In *La Consommation Collaborative*, Alain Decrop (ed.), Paris: De Boeck – Vuibert, pp. 169–189.

5. The prisoner's dilemma, enunciated in 1950 by Princeton University's Albert W. Tucker, characterizes in game theory terms a situation where two players ostensibly have an interest in cooperating, but where in the absence of any communication between the two, each will choose to betray the other if the game is played only once.

6. https://www.elle.com/culture/news/a37104/ruth-zukerman-flywheel-profile/

7. https://www.nytimes.com/video/business/100000004097143/soul-cycles-dynamic-duo.html

8. By permission of Kari Brandt.

9. By permission of Kari Brandt.

10. Victor W. Turner, *The Ritual Process: Structure and Antistructure*, Chicago, IL: Aldine, 1969.

11. https://www.goodcarbadcar.net/scion-brand-sales-figures-usa-canada/

12. https://www.mediapost.com/publications/article/87363/scion-seeks-community-in-new-campaign.html?edition=17666

7

EVOLVING FROM A COMMUNITY MOVEMENT TO AN ENTREPRENEURIAL PROJECT

An integrative case study would be the best way of illustrating the full range of potential actions explored in this book, if only because it shows how very important communities are to a successful project launch. Even if no perfect case study exists in the real business world, this chapter's analysis of the stage-by-stage approach to the process of building a community first and a start-up second is very useful since it identifies steps that all business founders are fully capable of taking intuitively (i.e. without necessarily being aware of what they are doing). It also looks at some of the more frequent challenges arising during this kind of entrepreneurial journey. After detailing the genesis of the BIMSTR project and the emergence of its Z'experts' community, the focus then turns to five essential steps already noted in previous chapters:

- advocating a cause and launching a movement;

- recruiting volunteers and organizing their collaboration;

- envisioning potential interactions between the people being mobilized in this way;

- developing rituals to sustain community life; and

- turning emotional connectivity into a central element in the value proposition.

ANICET, BIMSTR AND THE Z'EXPERTS' COMMUNITY

Created in 2015, BIMSTR[1] is a digital platform born out of an initiative taken by a group of young Cameroonians, starting with one of the authors of this book, Anicet Nemani, widely viewed as a digital communications expert not only because he masters all the salient concepts (including the management of online communities, the promotion of electronic word-of-mouth and the activation of social networks) but also because he knows many tricks of the trade helping to ensure a venture's effectiveness in this field. Nemani's experience in music promotions and digital background makes him quite unique in Africa and explains why he started an initiative seeking to unite all Cameroonian music fans – culminating ultimately in BIMSTR assuming and broader role and guaranteeing the viability of this entire genre.

BIMSTR started in 2015 with a simple WhatsApp group. This would be followed by a dedicated Cameroonian music Facebook page. It wasn't until the following year that the youth of this country really began following BIMSTR, which needed several months to upload content online before it started getting known. The trigger was Nemani's first video broadcast, 'The Views', a 9-minute long hit-parade that came online on 27 August 2016. His very specific style (called 'too deadly' in one comment) appealed to an initial audience that started to 'like' the video and follow the page. It was then that Nemani spontaneously said something that would ultimately become a rallying cry for Cameroonian music fans: 'Don't do witchcraft!', playing on the fact that anyone acting inappropriately tends in this country to be called a sorcerer. BIMSTR followers are therefore not supposed to partake in any witchcraft, meaning (in this context) that they are welcome to share music they like – even if this is the kind of thing that sorcerers might do. The whole narrative attracted a lot of people, with one commenting, 'We don't do witchcraft, we share things'. The whole trope became so widely used by followers that Anicet created hashtags like *#NeFaitesPasDansLaSorcellerie* ('Don't do witchcraft') and *#PartagezQuandCestBien*! ('Share it if it's any good') that would become very popular over time, with many Cameroonians constantly repeating them to one another. By year-end 2016, BIMSTR had more than 20,000 Facebook followers.

Unlike local mainstream media communications, all BIMSTR interactions are expressed in Cameroonian franglais, a hybrid local language mixing indigenous tongues, Pidgin-English, French and English. The idiom is an unassuming language used in popular circles. Note, for instance, two ways that people have of referring to their home country: KMER (because the assonance is similar); and 237 (the country code). Choosing to communicate in *Camfranglais* means that the community which BIMSTR is trying to federate sees the platform as an embodiment of cultural equality.

Nemani knew from the very outset that he did not have the expertise to appreciate the music at its true value. Having noticed that Cameroonians liked communicating via social networks to assert their identity, his solution was to give voice and power to his followers, farming out the burdensome task of judging and validating them. As these are not real experts, Nemani decided to call them 'Z'experts', a play on words translating his notion that they are akin to 'experts because like any good Cameroonian, they have an opinion on everything, but with a Z in front of their title, we can distinguish between them and conventional experts'.

The publications' writing style also become increasingly assertive:

> *Artists make music for the public, I think the audience's opinion is more important than our own. Dear Z'experts, do not hesitate to give your opinion, it's what counts .... At BIMSTR the customer is always right and Z'experts are our customers. Theirs are the only opinions that matter.*

All of which explains the speed with which Z'experts, with their role of 'sharing to inform' (and their willingness to comment on peers' discoveries), became such an essential link for Cameroonian artists. Whether they are in Cameroon or abroad, Z'experts can always be found collaborating online and opining on artists. They are similar to long-term volunteers, with many having collaborated for several years even if they sometimes need a break to concentrate on their studies or job. Not only have few left the community but the vast majority have become the nucleus of fans that BIMSTR needed to consolidate its position, with their increasingly frequent interactions and collaborations spurring the platform's development. Indeed, by 2020, more than 500,000 fans had subscribed to BIMSTR's Facebook page, on top of which it had 100,000 followers on Instagram plus more than 10,000 on Twitter. By April 2021, the numbers had reached 815,000 on Facebook and 154,000 on Instagram. In BIMSTR's conception, they are all Z'experts.

> *Z'experts are people who have subscribed to one or more of the BIMSTR pages on Facebook, Twitter, Instagram or You Tube. They operate without anyone knowing about them and engage either passively or actively. True Z'experts might share publications even before reading them. They often leave comments or 'like' something – but they never do witchcraft! Some also join Z'expert groups on Facebook, WhatsApp or Telegram. In any event and irrespective of what they do on BIMSTR platforms, Z'experts are mainly defined by their passion for culture in general and for 237 music in particular. (BIMSTR Facebook script)*

In just a few years, Nemani would build around the BIMSTR brand a thriving community that has become a key resource for generating economic activity.

CHAMPIONING A CAUSE AND STARTING A MOVEMENT

For the Facebook page to serve a unifying role, the project had to be positioned from the very outset as a social movement dedicated to the defence of Cameroonian music. As Nemani says, 'Our project actually calls for a wider struggle. It promotes not only our artists but also our national culture, which it validates and whose reputation it burnishes'. Moreover, many Z'expert community members support this cause explicitly. As the BIMSTR Facebook page says[2]:

> We are all Z'experts fighting for the same ideal: Culture 237 ... Our DNA is music and we express it through our 'likes', shares and comments ... [Our goal] is to continue to shine a light on Cameroon's culture, even as we continue to show respect for all the others.

BIMSTR is fully committed to defending 'KMER artists' and the '237 sound'. Whereas the rest of the local music world promotes other African or international genres, BIMSTR gives Z'experts a sense of being different. By sharing posts and comments on artists, the community plays a role in and supports the music industry. In a sense, Z'experts exist in opposition both to the music executives and the mainstream media outlets who have bombarded Cameroonians with foreign music. Z'experts' pride in participating in the BIMSTR project transcends its operational scope and resonates across the nation. Participants feel they are part of a collective effort to defend an endangered and undervalued national musical culture – and take great pride in this cause.

A Z'expert has spoken about how much she appreciates the BIMSTR project, saying that she supports 'everything that promotes Cameroon's digital development' due to her belief that the country's music sector has been 'abandoned' and now lags behind Nigeria or Ghana. Similarly, the Z'experts' Facebook page also features a comment from another Z'expert, who wrote, 'I appreciate the team's noble fight for Cameroon's artists (and culture in general). I'm always up for a noble fight!' Indeed, many Z'experts talk about fighting or struggling on behalf of their nation, a subliminal discourse that already existed before Nemani's project and which he succeeded in organizing and coordinating – to such an extent that BIMSTR's followers now view themselves as defenders of the national identity and attribute a national role to the project. In the words of a Z'expert from the beginning, 'BIMSTR is trying to save the nation ... and does this without receiving any financial aid or subsidies'. Similarly, another Z'expert avers that, 'In Cameroon today, we are getting re-acquainted with our own rhythms, returning to our roots, putting all our languages into the mix. BIM-STR has become a vector for progress'.

RECRUITING VOLUNTEERS AND ORCHESTRATING THE WORK THEY DO TOGETHER

BIMSTR operates by receiving unpaid assistance from Cameroonian music fans. There are two categories of helpers: 'volunteers' and 'Z'experts'.

BIMSTR has built its platform using volunteers, a small multidisciplinary group of about ten people from all sorts of backgrounds (computer scientists, designers, students and auto-didacts). All of this teamwork happens online. Some volunteers live in Cameroon; others are part of the Cameroonian diaspora living in Germany, France, England, Canada and the United States. The group is relatively stable and there have been very few departures (or arrivals) since 2016–2017. The difference between volunteers and Z'experts is that the latter are not part of the BIMSTR team and therefore unfamiliar with the strategy and concepts.

What BIMSTR mainly asks Z'experts to do is develop content from emerging Cameroonian musicians. Online collaborations are being organized at this level by Nemani, who assigns one task to each person, requesting for instance that they write a daily column or stream a weekly show. The whole point is to get people to share the things that they like the most and/or have discovered, while continuing to comment on whatever it is that fellow Z'experts have come up with. Z'experts are online all the time, collaborating on projects and administering their own Facebook group (called Z'experts' Community). Indeed, depending on their activities and the volume of materials they want to share, Z'experts are divided into different categories and receive badges recognizing the varying contributions they make.

Camille's story exemplifies the kinds of things that a BIMSTR volunteer can experience.[3] Originally from a working class neighbourhood in Yaoundé and a big fan of cinema, Camille did an internship at the IFC in her home city before being trained in reality television. She then shot her first professional film and created a *Ma Vision Ciné* page to talk about Cameroonian cinema. In 2015, she went on to do archive studies, specializing in Strategic Information at the University of Lyon III. By 2021, she was working as a communications and business intelligence officer in the Marseille office of an African fintech company selling a universal payment platform. Camille discovered BIMSTR when she got to Europe in late 2015 thanks to its fan base among compatriots who were already living there. After exploring the site for a while, she started meeting up with some of the artists listed there, listening to their music and spontaneously posting comments. People began tagging her posts to indicate that they had read them and it is this that kick-started what became a very productive relationship with BIMSTR. Camille now says that she found it natural to integrate the community, specifically because she wanted to become a Z'expert. She is now very active on a wide range of social networks.

In August 2017, Camille posted an opinion video on the BIMSTR website. An action that others might find innocuous is one she came to consider 'an honour' because she had done it specifically at Nemani's request. The video can still be found online. Then in October 2017, Nemani – in accord with the rest of the community – proposed a new collaboration involving the production of a weekly summary of all online Cameroonian urban music news – a programme to be called 'BIMSTR recap by Camille'. For five years now, Camille has been live on air for 45 minutes every Thursday evening at 9 p.m. (Cameroon time). She has made 150 videos and has more than a million views. Camille needs to 'concentrate when preparing her Thursday live show' and does not take this responsibility lightly. On top of this, between 2018 and 2020 she contributed to several major online events highlighting Cameroonian artists.

In Camille's view, Z'experts' collaboration on the BIMSTR platform is organized as follows: 'You decide yourself when you want a rest day. We have a workplace, the BIMSTR platform, and you can work 24/7 if you want'.[4] The reality is that Z'experts who want to contribute to BIMSTR but also have a job must find a way to balance their work schedule, breaks and time off. Camille would stress that Z'experts' 'main task is sharing'. The idea of a Z'expert's community is important at this level:

We all work for a culture we love enormously and which brings us together. Here, it's the music. Of course, Z'experts will sometimes clash, with each other or with volunteers. But we all maintain the same BIMSTR outlook.

Camille has said that like any Z'expert, she gets 'rewarded for performance, loyalty points plus things like super fan badges or concert tickets'. BIMSTR generally offers small rewards to Z'experts whose Facebook page has earned a 'super Z'expert' superfan badge due to the fact that they are online daily, commenting, sharing and 'liking' posts. Prizes include T-shirts or caps from BIMSTR and its partners, as well as Internet credits. In addition to these material rewards, Z'experts like Camille also get validation from other actions. One example is a laudatory January 2019 article written by Anicet and entitled. 'You're on BIMSTR all the time but still don't know Camille? You're lying like a politician'. In Camille's view, 'It was thanks to the Facebook article that I got my internship in Marseille', ultimately leading to a full-time job.

FOSTERING ONLINE AND OFFLINE INTERACTIONS

BIMSTR's digital platform has many tools it can use to promote community member interaction. The examples below are very different in nature. Firstly, there is the BIMSTR Challenge, which both increases interaction frequency and helps with the recruitment of new members. Otherwise, it is also worth noting Facebook tools like the Super Badge.

The BIMSTR Challenge

Launched in early January 2017, the BIMSTR Challenge tries to spotlight talented youth – whether or not they call themselves artists – while amplifying the platform's notoriety. Note this latter objective has already been met, with Jewanda (a cultural medium) writing in March 2017,[5] for instance, that, 'Within the space defined by its Challenge, BIMSTR's Facebook page is about to become the new favourite site for all Cameroon music lovers'.

The idea here is to have BIMSTR invite anyone with talent to produce a video where people sing either in *capella* or add beats to a Cameroonian song of their choice. As explained on the platform, 'You don't have to be professional or even dress up. It's open to everyone, even people who never thought about working as musicians'. The process is simple. After collecting 40 first-stage videos, a committee screens them for quality, irrespective of their origins (amateur or not). Twelve are selected and put into two groups for the rest of this three-round competition.

The first round involves voting by a Z'expert's jury formed for the occasion. This entails each member sharing the performances that they appreciate (with one share equal to one vote). Each video is then accompanied by the message, 'Only share what you dig. And remember, every time you share, you're adding a vote' – an instruction that echoes the famous hashtag from 2016, 'Don't do witchcraft'.

Grace's first video was posted on 15 February 2017 and sparked a blaze of 'likes' and discussions. The Z'experts' community all got behind the young woman, who was shared 5,800 times and received 2,100 comments. The video would be viewed 300,000 times on BIMSTR and generate a phenomenal buzz on social networks and other media. She then made another version for the semi-finals (3,700 'likes'; 675 comments) and a definitive version for the Grand Final (5,300 'likes'; 1,100 comments) – which she won.

In short, when the platform's journey began, the BIMSTR Challenge served as a real catalyst for interactions – explaining why its June 2018 renewal was no surprise.

Facebook's Super Fan Badge

Announced in late 2018 by the Mark Zuckerberg – the godfather of social networks – the Super Fan badge is an award bestowed upon a Facebook page's most active users, that is, individuals who view videos, 'like' photos and comment on posts. Facebook rewards these users for their loyalty and engagement by giving them a Super Fan badge that sets them apart from everyone else.

When subscribers to a Facebook page that is dedicated to a particular brand share and comment on its posts, they become readily identifiable as 'super fans' thanks to the juxtaposition of the badge with their username. The curious thing about this feature is that Facebook usurps the right to decide which fan of a page constitutes a super fan. The reality is that this reward takes advantage of the fan-brand relationship to enhance follower loyalty. When consumers receive a badge for following a page, they feel honoured and validated by the said brand. Because followers are proud to have been recognized, they will not want to disappoint the brand and/or lose a privilege that others do not possess. To keep the badge, they must therefore continue to interact daily on the pages where they are classified as fans, an outcome that ultimately suits everyone involved: Facebook; the brand; and members of the different communities involved, whose numbers grow all the time.

Having said that, little or no use has been made of this functionality in recent times. BIMSTR was quick to realize the advantage it could gain by further energizing its Z'expert community of African music enthusiasts. Hence the work done to regularly identify and highlight Super Z'expert fans, who also benefit from a host of game competitions, unifying events and one-off missions all relating to the brand's development. In turn, this has created a spirit of emulation that not only shines a light on Super Z'experts but also retains and even crystallizes the fan community surrounding BIMSTR. By understanding and applying these features over a six-month period, the platform grew from 145,000 to 175,000 subscribers, with the number of interactions revolving around fans' posts rising from 2 to 3 million.

DEVELOPING BIMSTR RITUALS

One thing that stands out when reading Z'expert Facebook posts is many members' ritual use of the phrase 'Don't do witchcraft'. It serves as a rallying cry that encourages action while defending Cameroonian artists – exemplified by one Jovani's 8 June 2019 Facebook post, 'Don't do witchcraft!! Go download African Subway. Encourage our kmer brothers'.

Other linguistic micro-rituals (like the *#237RaisonsDexceller* ['Reasons to Excel'] hashtag) always revolve around the things that connect community members to one another. There are also weekly rituals communicated through daily hashtags such as Monday's *#LundiStylé*, Wednesday's *#MercrediTout-EstPermis* ('Allow everything'), Thursday's *#JeudiConfession* or *#VendrediTchop*. With *#LundiStylé*, for instance, the community votes on members' style photos, with the winner receiving a voucher. One post from 29 June 2020 included the caption: 'It's *#LundiStylé* in our BIMSTR Community group. Members are all showing off their style with today's winner receiving a 20,000 CFA franc (US$35) voucher from the Zoé nails shop'. Not all micro-rituals include incentives, however, with *#JeudiConfession* invoking intimate confessions, for example, or *#VendrediTchop* seeing members post pictures of what they ate on the day.

In addition to these weekly micro-rituals publicizing community members' daily lives, macro-rituals are also celebrated, often relating to anniversaries like the creation of BIMSTR or Z'expert birthdays, culminating every time in an avalanche of posts featuring photos and/or videos. Macro-rituals of this kind will sometimes spread beyond the digital world and lead to community members gathering offline. One example is an annual football match between teams comprising Z'expert community members living in Yaoundé and their counterparts from Douala. This offline ritual is then shown online to increase all members' sense of belonging. After the 2019 match and at the same time as the Z'expert community was electing a president and celebrating the platform's sixth anniversary, the BIMSTR Facebook posted the following text accompanied by a slew of photos:

> *The football match organized by our Z'experts-labelled community was as beautiful as a groom's wedding suit. The match was played this morning at Douala's Elf Base under excellent conditions. It was one of the activities accompanying a Z'expert's organized gathering celebrating BIMSTR's sixth anniversary.*

MAKING CONNECTIVITY CENTRAL TO
THE VALUE PROPOSITION

BIMSTR went through all the stages of the community creation process and completed each one successfully. Yet the transition from its initial non-commercial community forms to today's commercialized activity was neither easy to predict nor to achieve. A trial-and-error approach tolerating a series of mis-steps was needed before the community could be instrumentalized into a value proposition that everyone would accept. Iterative entrepreneurial processes of this sort are essential for a project going through a business model's development phase.

The seminal idea here had been to take advantage of the absence of platforms diffusing or promoting Cameroonian music. As aforementioned, BIMSTR was using Facebook and WhatsApp to give people access to local music, helping fans discover a particular artist's discography but – and even more importantly – personal universe (favourite football team, influences, friends, diet, etc.). After two years of hard work, the founding entrepreneur and a small team of volunteer developers created a mobile app enabling Z'experts to listen to music similar to how people do with Spotify, and even buy it using Orange Money (since few pay by card in Cameroon). The idea was that by helping Cameroonian music fans stay in touch with their favourite artists, there might be less illegal downloading. The project never really took off, however, and even after several months of testing the results were disappointing.

The gap analysis was revised in 2019 and a decision made to change both the value proposition and the target market. The one advantage of the disappointment experienced until that point was that BIMSTR became aware of the extent to which future success depended on its community. Hence a new 'Revalt' ('Revalue The Target') concept, which recognized the importance of dynamism and interaction within the Z'expert community. The rejigged platform now gave consumer goods companies a chance to integrate active Z'expert community members directly into their social network communications strategies. BIMSTR began allocating funds to these Z'experts to help them fuse into a group capable of taking responsibility for co-creating BIMSTR's development – offering them formal recognition as bona fide counterparts, indispensable actors and key resources. The simple principle was that each Z'expert would henceforth share information or campaigns on any and all social networks with which they were acquainted, but also simultaneously with other community members.

BIMSTR Agency was born following this shift. Specializing in social media strategy, the new entity offered personalized support helping to develop people's social network presence. BIMSTR Agency relies heavily on Z'expert community members' communication strengths to bolster various one-off campaigns. It also serves as a community management training organization, helping to activate and federate community members online – especially on social networks. It is a talent incubator that has become a focal point for a number of young digital entrepreneurs looking to recruit staff. The training it provides helps to lift participants out of the spiral of unemployment by supporting their acquisition of new digital skills that they can then use to (re-)enter the labour market.

In short, BIMSTR's trial-and-error approach ultimately became a model – materialized in the creation of the social media agency – that differed from the one it had originally imagined. Even so, in and of itself the BIMSTR Agency did not automatically produce any linking value – this was achieved by the Z'experts' community working through the auspices of the BIMSTR platform. The commercial activity's impact on the community has been mainly positive (although this remains to be confirmed). On the other hand, there is also the possibility that the Agency's arrival has caused people to feel that their 'emotional labour' is being exploited.[6]

PROJECT FOUNDER FEEDBACK: TRANSITIONING FROM SEMINAL STRUGGLES TO *HOHAAA* MARKETING

This final section revisits the five stages of the process being discussed and takes a closer look at the problems arising when a community and a business are created in tandem. It is useful to be direct when discussing such matters, if only to gain a more granular understanding of the difficulties that Anicet Nemani experienced when founding BIMSTR. This focus on difficulties (especially relational ones) is justified by the many unpleasant surprises encountered during the project's development. (Note that the sub-section below is written in the first person to express the views of Anicet Nemani, BIMSTR project founder and co-author of this book).

Step 1 Challenges: Advocating a Cause and Starting a Movement

At first, when I only had a vague sense of what the BIMSTR project might become one day, I found it really hard to get people to join in my struggle. I started by contacting relatives (family and friends) to get their support, aware that I would not be able to do this all by myself. During this search phase, I would sometimes run up against staunch resistance, based on the general view that Cameroonians are unable to work together, with some people also wondering how long it would take them to get their money back. Above all, most believed that the project would die like so many other plans that people make.

Despite the frustration of all this rejection, I still felt a need to start writing the project plan. One thing led to another and I became more and more determined to defend the cause. I began viewing the project as a life struggle, indeed, this became a recurring theme for me. Then, when other people started gravitating towards my struggle, I realized that the movement is bigger than me alone. Especially because a lot more people became sincere about wanting to join the fight once my social media presence had expanded.

Step 2 Challenges: Recruiting Volunteers and Organizing Collaboration

Finding 'star' staff members has been crucial but also hard. Many young people found the BIMSTR project interesting and wanted to contribute. Almost all were willing to bring something extra to the table. Yet I needed to remain lucid and understand that I might get lost in the middle of all this goodwill; that having to manage everyone could be overwhelming; and that certain talents might not be optimal in helping me to launch the project. Hence my decision to make frequent use of volunteers, as long as they understand the vision, approach and strategy. Some are still here today, people I've been working with since the very beginning. Obviously, I've had other, less fortunate experiences with people who didn't really get the BIMSTR project's vision and even wanted to change it completely. Worse still, this also happened during some of the later development stages, after the project basis had already been established.

The BIMSTR project has volunteers living in many different countries and even continents. Most haven't met or known each other. The big challenge at this level has been getting them to connect. At BIMSTR, there needs to be a connection both between community members and between team members. The idea behind this approach is to ensure that team and community members open up to one another. Achieving this has required real long-term effort and inordinate availability; I have always made myself available to employees, catering to their needs, energizing our internal but also our external communities. We've had to find the right balance when spreading the work around – but also to ensure that the values being shared here are ones that will help us to work together. The hardest thing has been finding open spaces where team members can interact outside of a professional context. When people disagree, in the event of misunderstandings, my third party mediator role assumes a special meaning. It hasn't been possible for me to act in the same way as a manager does with their teams, or an entrepreneur with their employees. I'm always having to reach into my bag of tricks and use all kinds of tools to try and bring the temperature down and get people to refocus on project aims. My sole focus has been Z'expert team members. One surprise is the difficulties my friends and family have had in understanding my mindset and all the time I'm spending on the cause.

Step 3 Challenges: Fostering Online Interactions

It's hard developing a concept that everyone will like. The team and I have probably come up with something like 30 concepts, seven of which worked well. The constant challenge is to be resilient in case of failure, keeping things fresh and making sure that whatever idea works will continue to succeed over the long run. Here again, the community will not always agree with the vision or the specific objectives into which it's been broken down. Volunteers are pretty relaxed when discussing this but social network feedback can be pretty violent. With all the insults and harshness we get from some people, we regularly have to take a step back from things, keeping our distance and not responding impulsively. Having said that, most BIMSTR community members do agree with our main ideas and proposals.

Step 4 Challenges: Developing Rituals

The football match is one of our community's main rituals – without the shadow of a doubt. Z'experts play against other teams, including real clubs, wearing jerseys with the BIMSTR logo, which they pay for themselves. Some consider it a form of abuse because they are having to pay to promote BIMSTR, bolstering its image but not getting anything in return. On top of this, a rivalry has started between Douala and Yaoundé Z'experts to the point where the latter created a specific WhatsApp group that they then used to criticize BIMSTR management. To redress this, we had to revisit with them what a Z'expert's role entails and make it clear that the new WhatsApp group was undermining the BIMSTR spirit. You can't just let it ride when people are so hyped up about their rivalries that they forget we're supposed to be one big happy family. So we had to sort things out. But we did, for most everyone's benefit.

Step 5 Challenges: Making Emotional Connectivity a Core Element in the Value Proposition

It's important not to forget that the BIMSTR project is rooted in people's passion and driven by its social focus. We don't expect volunteers to be able to maintain the same level of commitment over time and aren't surprised when some eventually leave to refocus on their careers after having given us a few years of their time, expertise and sometimes even money. That's why we started twinning volunteers with our initial cohort of recruits, trying to achieve a better balance between everyone's efforts and obligations. Of course, this was also the period when I started experiencing greater commercial stress. Hiring a few more people would have been problematic given our budget, an issue that I admit I hadn't anticipated. Because the streaming platform doesn't really address economic imperatives, I thought of advertising on BIMSTR. That worked fairly well but not enough to ensure the project's future development.

Two main assets did play out as we expected, however: the BIMSTR community; and our social media skills. The end result has been the BIMSTR Agency, plus the consulting services we sell to a few major accounts and entrepreneurs. We mobilize our community to help launch different marketing actions that we then suggest to companies. What customers are buying here is the connection that exists between all community members. By partnering with BIMSTR to run their social media campaigns, they are able to incorporate much greater linking value into their product or service offer. One example is the contract we were awarded by Cameroon's leading company for the production, distribution and marketing of mineral water, beer, energy drinks, soft drinks and non-carbonated beverages, commissioning us to manage the entire TOP soft drink product range across all the different social networks.

General awareness of the effectiveness of the marketing approach being deployed under the BIMSTR banner has sparked a whole new rallying cry for marketing in Cameroon, one that has come to be known as *Hohaaa* marketing. The word is a *Camfranglais* expression meaning 'by force'. *Hohaaa* marketing mixes tribal and content marketing and makes followers the key element in this domain – attesting to the importance of coupling community and entrepreneurial activities with one another.

NOTES

1. https://www.facebook.com/bimstr237/

2. https://www.facebook.com/bimstr237/

3. By permission of Camille Owono.

4. By permission of Camille Owono.

5. https://www.jewanda.com/2017/03/reseaux-sociaux-deux-jeunes-camerounais-enflamment-toile-reprise-dadele/

6. Arlie R. Hochschild, *The Managed Heart: Commercialization of Human Feeling*, Los Angeles, CA: University of California Press, 1983.

8

COMMUNITY 1ST – START-UP 2ND

To better understand how and why entrepreneurs might look to foster a community before starting up a business – a process reversing their usual modus operandi – it is important to identify key questions that company founders must ask themselves when preparing each of the five stages comprising this process. Towards this end, the chapter formulates guidelines representing crucial milestones in this process, steps that – if sufficiently monitored – should ensure the success of any corporate venture built around a brand community.

Success is never guaranteed, first and foremost because it can mean different things from one individual to the next. Having said that, entrepreneurs tend to have greater success when they are capable of fulfilling a community's aspirations while embedding the transition of their business in a value proposition that community members will favour. Even so (and notwithstanding numerous examples offered in this book), negotiating the aforementioned process stages can be challenging – especially when other issues arising outside of (or even after) the process must be addressed, problems that relate to the future growth of a company and/or its brand and which often tend to occur years after the launch, irrespective of any initial successes it might have had. Problems of this nature tend to distance the business founder (and the company itself) from the community – and vice versa, subsequently. The chapter concludes with two cases studies representing diametrically opposed situations, both of which speak to this very important moment in the post-process management of a brand or business.

GUIDELINES: KEY PROCESS STAGE FACTORS

The guidelines below cover the five process stages detailed throughout this book relating to the way a project founder might foster a community before subsequently launching a start-up:

1. Advocating a cause and launching a movement.

2. Recruiting volunteers.

3. Fostering interaction and sharing stories.

4. Developing rituals.

5. Inserting linking value into the value proposition.

Stage 1 Milestones: Advocating a Cause and Launching a Movement

This first step is crucial and requires a complete reversal of perspective. Putting the community before one's own business is something that many aspiring entrepreneurs find difficult, if only because it forces them to focus less on problem-solving per se and more on the issue of which causes are worth defending. The creativity and brainstorming sessions relating to this question that the authors of this book have carried out with potential project founders often end up with a whole host of ideas about solutions – and very few about causes. Yet to build the foundations for a community, it is at this stage that a cause must formulated, whether or not it is new.

The person initiating the advocacy of the cause should not be trying at this juncture to respond to a specific need but instead raising awareness of a cause that will have to be constructed before it can consolidate. This applies particularly where health and environmental causes are concerned. In situations as controversial as these, a cause's defence will begin with an investigation seeking to reconstruct the chain of causality, verify damages and demonstrate how the problem affects different categories of people, animals, plants, etc. In some instance, the demonstration serves to recognize problems whose reality has been contested or denied. In others, it is less the problems' reality that sparks debate and more the question of their origin. Hence the need for in-depth scrutiny when first formulating the advocacy of a cause, an initial step that can subsequently translate into a real investigation.

Before seeking (and obtaining) support for these efforts, people must first be made aware of everything at stake and understand why they are being asked to get involved. The cause triggers mobilization by stabilizing the reasons why an action must be taken, with stakeholder support being viewed at this level as a resource ensuring the durability thereof. As noted in Chapter 2, the cause is often communicated via a manifesto, a word derived from Latin with a connotation of something very clear and noteworthy. Even though manifestos vary in terms of their length and contents, when compiled thoughtfully and convincingly they can both attack a given worldview and suggest practical ways of achieving certain objectives. Starting with an attention-grabbing sentence is generally a good way of getting people's attention.

The essential characteristic of a manifesto is the fact that it always conveys a message. Not only must this message exist but it must be explicit; communicate the manifesto's *raison d'être*; be clear (i.e. manifested) and open for everyone to see – even if subtexts can be useful. First comes the message and then comes the presentation thereof. Factors like the interpretation of events, the choice of historical data or the conscious or unconscious omission of variables (representing a decision to mask, conceal or camouflage the message) are also just as important in getting the target audience to adhere to the cause as to the message itself. Manifestos do not speak to isolated individuals but to the members of a prospective community. They often use the first-person plural – the pronoun 'we' – from the very outset to evoke a collective dimension.

Manifestos rally support for the cause that is being defended, helping in this way to launch a movement that must, in turn, have a name which will ultimately become its brand. The name chosen for members of the movement must also be self-referential. Otherwise, the movement should assume a variety of forms to make it easier for supporters to gather. The rise of the Internet has spawned less formalized forms of movements, exemplified by Facebook or Instagram pages as well as all kinds of blogs. People use blogs to fight a wide range of injustices, including wrongful imprisonment, government corruption, environmental degradation and human rights abuses. Blog advocacy[1] occurs when a blog is used to champion a cause. Other forms of movement exist as well, starting with non-profit associations.

Lastly, definitions for these crucial points can be complemented by an action plan detailing the movement's ambitions and stages of progress.

The questions that might be asked during Phase 1 include:

1. What cause is being defended?

2. Why are people defending this cause?

3. Which people, animals or other parties are being defended?

4. What is noteworthy about the manifesto's introductory sentence (shock value)?

5. Which data and events are being challenged in the manifesto?

6. What is the movement's name (brand)?

7. What are members of the movement called?

8. What form did the movement take at first? Blog? Social media page? Non-profit? etc.

9. Which actions (petitions, consultations, events, meetings, interventions, etc.) are being planned to bring people together and help the cause to grow?

Stage 2 Milestones: Recruiting Volunteers

Project founders maintain during Phase 2 the reverse perspective that they originally adopted for the first, conceptualizing in terms of volunteers rather than employees. The idea is not to offer generous pay to attract competent candidates but to convince people to join the cause of their own volition and do it for free. This is because their support and commitment will be indispensable to some of the activities that the movement is planning. Founders cannot and should not try to do everything by themselves.

Of course, volunteers thinking about joining a cause will need motivation, the first vector of which is the intrinsic value that they attribute to the cause. On top of this, there may be extrinsic motivational factors, starting with the search for identity. Many people feel that advocating a cause helps them to feel good about themselves and get other people to also think well of them. Otherwise, the desire for personal fulfilment, to develop new skills or to enrich one's resume are further motivational factors.

There are two categories of volunteers. The first might become the project founder's pretorian guard, being the group that helps the leader to manage the movement. Then comes an army of volunteers prepared to defend the cause and participate in all of the on- and offline actions publicizing it, thereby attracting even more followers. In short, different kinds of tasks and roles will end up being assigned to different categories of volunteers.

For a movement launched online in the guise of an advocacy blog,[2] there needs to be a pretorian guard of competent volunteers overseeing the assignment of management roles and tasks. These include:

- *Writers*: frequently posting the latest news about the cause.

- *Coders*: altering, if need be, a blog's stylistic aspects (font, background colour, etc.) and creating widgets like animated blog badges.

- *Designers*: using advanced skills to produce graphic presentations and videos.

- *Networkers*: maintaining contacts with journalists and other bloggers.

- *Translator(s)*: translating the blog into other languages.

With the pretorian guard of competent volunteers carrying out these roles and tasks, it behoves other volunteers driven by their own enthusiasm to assume the roles and tasks involved in mobilizing the movement and expanding the community. These include:

1. *Evangelizers*: inspiring new people to follow the movement and defend the cause.

2. *Hosts*: welcoming new movement followers and assigning roles to them.

3. *Facilitators*: organizing events and assigning simple tasks.

4. *Storytellers*: telling uplifting stories about the cause and its founder.

5. *Supporters*: participating in all advocacy events.

The questions that might be asked during Phase 2 include:

1. How are community volunteers referred to?

2. What levers above and beyond the cause itself can be used to motivate volunteers?

3. What kinds of profiles do different volunteers have?

4. What are volunteers' respective roles/tasks/activities?

5. How should evangelized followers be referred to?

Stage 3 Milestones: Fostering Interactions and Sharing Stories

With different categories of volunteers having been recruited, a community is now ready to emerge, with the focus shifted to helping members interact via activities enhancing their commitment and dedication to the cause, hence their sense of community. Without interaction, there can be no community.

One simple way to foster interaction is to have stories to share. Project founders have a big role to play at this level by telling their own story (and history) such as it relates to the cause. The more their past explains their closeness and commitment to the cause, the more their stories will be deemed 'authentic' and spark word-of-mouth between volunteers and followers. To repeat, founders must refrain from talking about solutions (and especially about products or other offers) and instead share personal titbits. Only then can they ask volunteers to do the same.

Project founders and volunteers are not the only persons capable of producing material via word-of-mouth. Once the movement has succeeded in getting participants to gather on- and/or offline, it becomes possible for the community to share memories using stories or visuals (photos or videos), with online exchanges of this nature reinforcing offline advocacy events. Note that even with causes of the utmost gravity, playful events like challenges or intra-member battles can be useful.

Hashtags – considered nowadays as a perfect way of rallying people digitally – can accelerate the sharing of volunteer- and follower-generated content. Project founders can invite community members to more or less stage their cause advocacy, for instance, by sharing photos adorned with hashtags in a way that synthesizes the scene they are staging.

The questions that might be asked during Phase 3 include:

1. What kinds of authentic stories might a project founder tell and share?

2. What off- and/or online events might be created to get a community to gather?

3. How is an events-related sharing of contents best supported?

4. Does the cause lend itself to intra-member challenges, battles, etc.?

5. Which hashtags are most likely to increase the number of interactions?

Stage 4 Milestones: Developing Rituals

Project founders must not only facilitate member interaction but also bolster their sense of belonging to a community that expresses and perpetuates itself through members' participation in collective rituals. The latter comprises an ordered sequence of behaviours that is more rigid and more predictable than an ordinary action.

Its pattern also repeats over time. The project founder must develop and spread two main types of rituals: micro and macro.

Micro-rituals are brief episodes where someone is recognized for their membership in a community. Examples include making a specific gesture when meeting a fellow member, or everyone doing the same thing with the same object at the same time of day. Even the simplest of rituals can be very meaningful for members, involving objects that range from the most mundane (wearing a bracelet, scarf, headband, etc.) to high tech (i.e. smartphones, motor vehicles). The only requirement is that the objects in question bear the movement's brand name.

Macro-rituals are gatherings that recur regularly (weekly, monthly, annually) and 'force' members to be present and interact as per specific patterns. They must also bolster people's sense of belonging to something larger than themselves. The project founder must ensure that the macro-ritual revolves around an episode that both relates to the cause being defended and is also relatively playful in nature (choreography, parades, song, games, balloons, etc.). The date chosen for the macro-ritual must also be meaningful to the cause.

Another crucial aspect is the sequencing of rituals, which should be neither too easy nor too hard for community members to do. Project founders must always bear in mind that members are not there to cogitate upon the ritual but simply to perform it, explaining their general reliance on volunteers who will have already integrated its codification. The latter can then serve as masters of ceremony when the first ritual is held, helping all the other members to perform it.

The questions that might be asked during Phase 4 include:

1. Which micro-rituals need to be developed?

2. Which object should be used during these micro-rituals?

3. Which macro-ritual needs to be developed? At what juncture?

4. How is the macro-ritual to be structured? How is it to be sequenced?

5. Which volunteers should be involved in performing the macro-ritual?

Stage 5 Milestones: Inserting Linking Value
into the Value Proposition

It is once the cause advocate community has been fostered and consolidated that the movement initiator looks at capitalizing upon this group of adherents to start a company. It is a transition that can be difficult for community members accustomed to a non-commercial context – although it may also be something that they expect and have even requested because they want (and are willing to pay for) a product, experience or brand reaffirming their sense of belonging.

'Monetizing' a community created to defend a cause – concretizing the revenue model – is a crucial step for business founders. This should in no way be taken to mean that they themselves are going to stop defending the cause but instead that they will be fusing the community with a commercial activity whose brand name clearly signifies its connection to the movement advocating the cause. To align with community members' own experiences, the commercial activity – regardless of whether it involves a product, service, experience or brand – must offer linking value that helps people to build, develop and/or maintain a connection to one another.

When considering how to inject connectivity into a (company's) commercial activity, the real question is the best way of getting the product or service offer to invigorate the intra-personal inter-action that is the starting point of all linking value. Everything that a company offers serves to facilitate different types (i.e. emotional, physical, playful) of interactions conceptualized first in terms of what they mean to community members, and then to non-members.

To capitalize on a community (which, to repeat, comes first in this approach, before the business itself), a project founder must reject the suggestion made far too often in marketing guidebooks that isolated individual consumers should be targeted by whatever product, service or brand is on offer. Restricting a start-up's value proposition to this one single focus risks squandering all the movement and community capital that it will have taken so much time to accumulate. Instead, the value proposition must be framed in terms of its linking value – a difficult shift for anyone coming out of the business, management and marketing worlds but still the right thing to do if only because it perpetuates the reversal perspective underling the first process stage – and by so doing enacts the singular approach that is specified all throughout this book.

The questions that might be asked during Phase 5 include:

1. What do community members need in order to solidify their sense of belonging?

2. Towards this end, do they require a product, service or experience?

3. What kind of offering fits this need, and to what extent does it facilitate interaction?

4. How capable is this offering of attracting people who are not community members?

5. What is the brand name of the commercial activity being proposed?

POST-LAUNCH, THE COMMUNITY WILL BE BOTH ESSENTIAL BUT ALSO BURDENSOME

Once the activity is underway – bearing a brand name reminiscent of the movement created to defend the cause (and featuring a value proposition that emphasizes linking value) – the business founder can use the community for market testing, demonstration and communication purposes. In this sense, the latter helps the former achieve commercial success. Of course, the risk here is that the community will feel betrayed if it suspects that it is being instrumentalized for commercial reasons alone and conceivably turn against the project founder in that case.

To understand the potential problem arising outside of (and following) the processes described in this book, the present chapter concludes with a synoptic narrative of two cases that are diametrically opposed in terms of their post-launch stories and subsequent commercial success.

Glossier: When a Company Detaches
From Its Community

Earlier chapters have already referred to the example of Glossier, created by Emily Weiss in 2014, four years after she started her blog, 'Into the Gloss'. Until now, analysis has focused on her 'Community first, Business second' approach, plus the community-to-business transition that she led from 2010 to 2020. What is striking about the years since then is the alienation felt by Glossier's community when it sensed an over-emphasis on commercial interests.

Glossier had sparked a great deal of excitement in early 2019 when its Instagram feed published a mysterious post alluding to an intriguing new product line. The whole campaign – first teased out in a February 22 post before the official launch 11 days later on 4 March – drove online fans wild speculating about various brand extension possibilities (including activewear and sex toys). When it turned out that the big news involved little more than a new range called Glossier Play and comprised dialled-up beauty extras and evening-oriented beauty products, the community was underwhelmed, immediately inundating the company's Instagram account with disappointed comments highlighting problems like the fact that the new Glitter Gelée eyeshadow had environmentally problematic ingredients. As one fan wrote, 'Well. That was under-whelming. Weeks of hype for a bloody pencil sharpener and some glitter'.[3] In December 2020, Glossier emailed its whole communi-ty to announce that the product range would be discontinued on 4 January 2021. Glossier Play was, in short, a flop: first, because the product contained a glittery gel with non-biodegradable flakes; but also because each product delivery used an almost indecent amount of plastic and/or aluminium packaging. Most Glossier community members actively disliked the new product range and took offence at the brand's blatant disregard for sustainability. Following numer-ous consumer complaints, Glossier did reduce the amount of pack-aging used for its Play range but this was a case of too little, too late. The big picture is that the Glossier community was put off by the new launch, wondering why the brand was now pushing coloured make-up given its seminal message about the value of acting natu-rally. Community members' loyalty to Glossier had been based on the idea that make-up is not meant to make people beautiful but instead to accentuate their natural beauty, a cause that specifically precludes the idea of artificialization (such as coloured make-up). By altering its produce offer as it did, Glossier put itself at odds with its community's sustainability expectations and values.

Glossier's net valuation in July 2021 was $1.8 million after raising $80 million that month to further develop its global digital channels and retail outlets. Three new stores were opened in Seattle, Los Angeles and London, first steps in a new expansion strategy that the company said would revolve around a combination of e-commerce-based market entries, along with the addition within a few short years of dozens of new stores in the United States and elsewhere:

> *Now, nearly seven years into Glossier's journey, our strategy and the expectations of beauty consumers everywhere are aligned: beauty discovery increasingly begins online as people look for inspiration from friends and strangers alike, and customers want to move fluidly between immersive and personalized e-commerce and retail experiences. This is the future we've always been building for.*[4]

Many fans were surprised by the new direction, viewing it as a biased interpretation of what the community wanted. Indeed, for some it was the very opposite. To them, the discourse sounded like the kind of strategy talk that global company would engage in, something far removed from the empathetic words they expected from Emily Weiss, who they had once considered the leader of their community – being a person who at the outset of Glossier's journey had once responded to a question about beauty industry advertising tropes by saying, 'At Glossier, we're not going to make a commercial with wind-billowing satin, like a unicorn whispering luxury'.

The Glossier community was further shaken by a January 2022 decision to fire 80 employees (one-third of the workforce, mainly technology staff), due to the company having allegedly over-hired. Weiss said;

> *We're making these changes to effectively execute what we are uniquely suited to do at Glossier: cultivate a brand that inspires our community, deliver magical and unique*

experiences, and create essential beauty products that our customers can use for a lifetime.[5]

But the community was not on-board with the measure, finding it impossible to justify 80 employees losing their job at a time when the company had just raised $80 million. Ex-fans of Glossier – now its adversaries – accused the brand of venality and forgetting the passion it had once felt for its community.

Filoni: Ongoing Symbiosis With a Community

Whereas the Glossier case study is the story of a project founder after first building a brand community instrumentalized it to fulfil pure business interests, Filoni is the story of a budding entrepreneur's initial reliance on a community built around an existing activity. According to Interbrand's latest report – Breakthrough Brands 2020[6];

The new generation of brands is putting the community at the core of its identity from the start ... Some are building businesses to serve thriving subcultures, while others are nurturing community through built-in interactive options.

Filoni was created to serve a community subculture, in this case, fans of spelunking.

Gianni Filoni hails from a small mountain village between Italy's Tuscany and Emilia Romagna regions. His love for the great outdoors saw him spend a great deal of time exploring local mountain ranges, often together with family and friends. From these experiences soon emerged a real passion for spelunking, a subset of mountaineering that involves the exploration of cliffs and caves. Filoni's passion was something he shared with a local community of enthusiasts, crystallized in a local community called the Mountain Speleologist Group (MSG).

MSG members were unhappy with some of their existing tools, which they knew were not safe enough. A big issue was the need for drills to make holes for nails that they could then use to climb or descend walls and tunnels. Extreme weather conditions (i.e. severe temperature changes) tended to cause the battery-operated and electric drills currently on the market to both lose their charge quickly. What people needed was a reliable, light-weight and easy to hand drill that would work in caves, that is, far from any power sources. To solve this problem, Filoni and two colleagues came up with the idea of combining a fuel-powered brush cutter motor that was already on the market with another company's hammer (being the technologically most important component, hence the one at greatest risk in difficult operating conditions). The first prototype they created, which fit these two components to a motherboard and attached a power transmission belt, was tested live to fine-tune its technical, ergonomic and functional properties. Everyone was extremely positive after Filoni showed them how to use his first prototype drill. Indeed, they wanted to buy one immediately.

The first prototype was followed by a second and then a third that was similarly tested in the field for other properties such as weight distribution, grip, handling, situational applicability, etc. Manufacturing then began, with the company selling the new product under the brand name of Stone Drill, emphasizing the uniqueness of a drill powered by its own fuel source instead of electricity, as is generally the case? MSG members were the first to use Stone Drill, which then expanded to a wider fan community. In Filoni's words;

> Stone Drill would never have been born without the caving group and the passion and experiences shared with them. It was this local group that started the word-of-mouth that eventually reached the broader community of Italian cavers. ... My new product created an immediate buzz, which gave me the energy to continue.[7]

A whole range of Stone Drill products would be designed under the supervision of Filoni, tasked with developing innovative ideas within the confines of his father's company. Significantly wider professional opportunities also began arising with civil defence and Alpine rescue customers, who had heard about the new product through an infectious word-of-mouth. In the end, Stone Drill would ultimately be sold internationally. Despite this evolution, today Gianni Filoni still sees the Stone Drill product range – derived from his MSG experience – as preserving the original spelunking connection, if only because the product would not have existed without the community or the knowledge derived from his early experiences. Filoni has always dedicated a great deal of time and effort to MSG community life, a devotion recognized by all concerned. Indeed, he still enjoys a reputation as a very active member who gives much to others, that is, he is not viewed as a free rider taking advantage of his community to develop his own international business interests.

The contrast between Glossier and Filoni shows how communities locked into a 'Community first, Start-up second approach' can be both indispensable and burdensome. In the former case, the community had been the motor behind a successful commercial activity before detaching itself from (and even opposing) a project founder accused of becoming over-ambitious commercially. In the latter, the risk for a business founder who never betrayed his community was weaker commercial growth than might have otherwise been the case. The lesson here is that it is useful for a project founder to provide support and coaching during all of the five stages studied in this chapter, while also taking a step back to (re) think about the community connection and asking at what point such relationships tip into a commercial activity.

NOTES

1. https://advox.globalvoices.org/wp-content/downloads/gv_blog_advocacy2.pdf

2. https://advox.globalvoices.org/wp-content/downloads/gv_blog_advocacy2.pdf

3. https://snobette.com/2020/02/glossier-shuts-down-glossier-play-launch-was-a-flop/

4. https://uk.fashionnetwork.com/news/Glossier-secures-80-million-in-funding-ahead-of-physical-relaunch,1317840.html

5. https://ww.fashionnetwork.com/news/Glossier-lays-off-80-employees, 1372912.html

6. https://interbrand.com/thinking/breakthrough-brands-2020/

7. S. Guercini & B. Cova, "How innovation nurtures well-being in enthusiast communities." *Innovation: Organization & Management*, 24(4), 522–551, 2022.

9

ACHIEVING A DIFFERENT KIND
OF ENTREPRENEURSHIP

This book has up until now detailed five steps for structuring the joint creation of a community and a start-up, illustrated by a number of case studies. All these phases have been designed to occur before a company's business model is formalized, setting up this final chapter to answer two questions: how a community model might be incorporated into a business model: and how the two models might coexist to ensure that a company achieves durable growth in both commercial and non-commercial terms.

After a brief description of the two approaches that have been widely instrumentalized over the past decade by many entrepreneurs intent on developing their own business models, analysis revisits salient dimensions of the community model before detailing the integrative and/or combinatory cycles that govern these two models at the point where they converge – specifically in light of the social value proposition that each offers. The conclusion then evokes a number of statutory forms that can be applied to these new entrepreneurial organizations in a context defined by the support they receive from their respective communities.

CONTRIBUTIONS AND LIMITATIONS OF
THE BUSINESS MODELS

The section following is neither intended to revisit the origins of business models, nor their various definitions. Instead, it simply seeks to present certain constituent dimensions thereof.

The Business Model Canvas: Putting a Value
Proposition at the Heart of a Business Model

In their book entitled *Business Model Generation*,[1] Alexandre Osterwalder and Yves Pigneur construct an entire approach around a business model framework that is generally considered essential in contemporary entrepreneurship. Comprising nine blocks[2] (enunciated below), the tool facilitates the adoption of a common language.

This highly dynamic canvas includes:

- a value proposition aligned with customer needs;

- a company's target segments;

- the channels used to sell and deliver products/services to customers and to communicate with them. These correspond to different customer contact points;

- customer relationships, describing the nature and type of relations that the company wants to establish with its various targets;

- key resources (skills) enabling the company to create value and to offer it to customers, in order to sustain relations with them;

- key activities that a company must perform if its business model is to succeed;

- partnerships with networks of suppliers and external counterparts;

- the company's revenue stream; and

- the costs involved and incurred when creating and delivering products/services.

The value proposition lies at the heart of the business model canvas. The centrality of its role is what prompted the book's authors to specifically focus on value proposition design[3] within a few short years after publishing their first bestseller. Of course, these dimensions cannot be considered without taking their inter-relationships into account.

Lean Canvas: Iterative Dynamics Associated With a Business Model

Éric Ries's book *The Lean Start-up*[4] has suggested that the philosophy of lean management[5] be adapted to organizations' actual entrepreneurial and innovation processes. Starting with the observation that a business model's most noteworthy evolution occurs during the early stages of a company's life, the author has developed a new methodology revolving around the relatively short time cycles that allow companies in the process of being created to rapidly adjust their model, if need be. These cycles are organized into three main phases: Build; Measure and Learn. Whenever a company is born, it necessarily comes with a whole set of ideas that will have to be tested as soon as possible. Among these ideas are two of the assumptions that any and all entrepreneurs make: a value hypothesis; and a growth hypothesis. The former makes it possible to test whether a product delivers real value to customers once it is used. The latter tests how the company intends to discover and attract new customers.

The goal here is to experiment with these hypotheses as soon as possible by developing an early summative version of the product/service and then distributing it to early adopters (Build). The purpose is to quickly apprehend what customers want and to ensure that the company offers a solution to any problems that may arise. Towards this end, Ries suggests that organizational metrics be devised to monitor (Measure) what needs to be learned. These have to be:

- actionable, that is, clearly demonstrate the causes and effects of what is being measured;
- accessible, that is, be as simple as possible; and
- audible, that is, so that any data collected is credible to employees.

In short, developing and using these metrics teaches organizations whether they need to review their basic assumptions and pivot strategically or else if they should persevere (Learn). Given this lean dynamic, the lean canvas extends Osterwalder and Pigneur's business model, focusing on the learning process while validating start-ups' underlying hypotheses. The process may be closely tied to a company's customer segments but like the business model canvas, it does not account for the very real contributions potentially offered by a community of customers developed upstream from the business model. By mobilizing the community and volunteers right from the outset, entrepreneurs can shorten iterative cycles, limit the number thereof and even co-create products, services and experiences.

The simplified representation proposed by these various business models creates meaning and makes it possible to convince and reassure any stakeholders who might otherwise be daunted by the project's uncertainty. It also formalizes the company that the entrepreneur is trying to found. With this in mind, the business model might best be understood as a tool that is as strategic as it is operational – hence useful, because it encompasses the strategic importance of stakeholders (including customers) as well as the possibility of generating collective meaning. This is redolent of constructs mobilized throughout this book, including 'causes' and 'movements'.

All in all, the business model concept enhances understanding of how a company creates, delivers and captures value. The way it has been represented – via the business model canvas and the lean canvas – reveals the importance of stakeholders and the roles they play in an organization. This focus is sufficiently open for the model to incorporate into the entrepreneurial approach something that it has lacked until now, namely the community dimension, redressing a lack of emphasis heretofore on either community power or the leadership role that customers, in the guise of brand volunteers, are capable of performing.

COMMUNITY MODELS IN THE SERVICE OF ENTREPRENEURIAL PROJECTS

Unlike business models, community model constructs have undergone less development over the years. As noted in Chapter 1, to exist a community must possess three essential characteristics:

1) awareness of forming a separate group;
2) existence of rituals and traditions; and
3) a moral obligation to provide mutual assistance.

To build up a community featuring these fundamental characteristics, some organizations have adopted a framework originally developed for business models, using it to either create tools conducive to the launch of a new community or else to analyse and improve upon an existing one. Such canvases are guides helping to identify basic issues and ask useful questions.

A first community canvas proposed by the Community Canvas Project[6] has been organized into three main sections centred on questions crucial to community development:

- *Identity*: Who are we and what do we believe in? Strong communities have a clear and explicit understanding of who they are, why they exist and what purpose they serve. Key questions for them are their *raison d'être* and who qualifies as a member.

- *Experience*: What happens in the community and how does it create value for members? How can the community's purpose be transformed into tangible value? Two types of experience matter at this level: shared experiences uniting members and strengthening their bonds; and regular individual experiences possessing a strong symbolic dimension.

- *Structure*: Which elements provide long-term stability? Many communities may be born spontaneously but few survive over the long run. The organizational aspects are often neglected and do not necessarily possess the structures allowing them to respond to whatever new issues will inevitably arise and become key episodes in the community's further development.

A second community canvas developed by Microsoft[7] incorporates nine dimensions that community founders should master:

- *Raison d'être*: Why does the community exist? What cause is it defending? How does it differ from other communities?

- *Members*: How do community members define themselves? What typifies members' profiles? How do they differ from members of other communities? How do they recognize one another?

- *Values*: What matters to community members? What are they most likely to reject out of hand? What do members view as a counter-model?

- *Aims*: In what terms is the advocacy of a cause being expressed (i.e., 'Save French underpants')? What short- and medium-term objectives are being pursued through the community movement being created in this way? How are outcomes to be measured?

- *Experiences*: What do members share with one another? What do they experience in common? Which micro- and macro-rituals mark community life?

- *Roles*: What variety of roles do community members play? What tasks are being delegated to members in light of these roles? Which specific tasks are delegated to volunteers?

- *Rules*: What are the rules governing interactions between members? What rules of politeness are in place? How are inactive members dealt with?

- *Governance*: How are decisions made regarding the future of the community? Are any community subgroups authorized to make decisions autonomously?

- *Communication*: What language does the community use? What are members' preferred means of communication, both among themselves and with the outside world?

Like business models, the different community models complement one another and converge to help describe and qualify a community. Even so, they tend to provide little information on how to build, run, develop and maintain the community that they have qualified.

Within this context, the five-step approach that this book proposes constitutes a significant contribution to the debate. More specifically, it suggests concrete solutions to a range of 'how' questions: how to start a cause and begin organizing a movement; how to recruit volunteers; how to interact with one's community both online and offline; how to nurture rituals and how to inject connectivity into a future business model's value proposition.

The community precedes the business model but also helps to shape it. The question then becomes how the two models might be combined and helped to coexist at each stage of the newly created company's development.

THE DOUBLE TEMPORALITY OF COMMUNITY AND COMPANY DEVELOPMENT

An entrepreneurial approach always happens within a given timeframe, one that tends to materialize through trial and error. Entrepreneurs sometimes doubt themselves and will learn from their mistakes. Learning is central to any successful venture, notwithstanding the fact that it requires a central idea, guidelines and a strategic framework. In other words, the entrepreneur's vision is destined to be translated into the company's mission and then broken down into specific objectives that must be achieved. At the same time, self-learning of this kind needs to be sustained by both the community and the business model.

Incorporating this dual temporality is therefore one way of supporting an entrepreneurial venture. The first timeframe is materialized through community members' adhesion to the project – a useful way of driving its ultimate transition into a corporate form. The clear objective is therefore that both these temporalities be able to coexist so that the two models can enrich one another. Of course, the company will then take precedence over the community, potentially by instrumentalizing early (or even later) followers and regenerating a holy flame. Schematically, the two models can be combined into four phases (see Fig. 1):

- The first phase involves the community's emergence but little else. It incorporates the steps outlined in Chapters 2–5 (Advocating for a cause and starting a movement – Recruiting volunteers – Fostering interactions and sharing stories – Developing rituals). The phase can last from a few weeks to several years depending on the circumstances. The advent of the entrepreneurial venture marks the end of this first phase, being the point when connectivity is integrated into the future company's value proposition.

- The second phase sees the community develop and consolidate on the back of the movement launched during the initial phase. Digital platforms become paramount, as witnessed by the

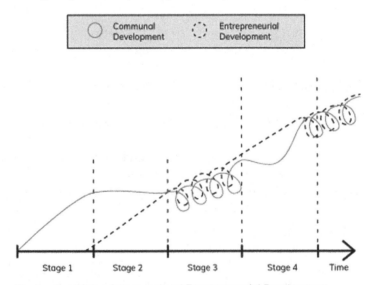

Fig. 1.   Combining Communal and Entrepreneurial Development.
Source: Authors.

'Into the Gloss' and BIMSTR case studies. The entrepreneurial project takes shape either constantly or, more often, through trial and error. In any event, the end of this phase is marked by a convergence between the business and community models, manifested in the form of a value proposition that incorporates the community link (as Chapter 6 explained).

• The third phase gets the two models to work together, with each nurturing the other. The more the business grows, the more the community flourishes thanks to the company's linking value. The more the community grows, the more it strengthens consumers' brand loyalty. This virtuous circle sees the entrepreneur iterate with the community in an attempt to design new offers and create the new rituals that community life requires. Community members' skill sets are essential both to the success of business and to community life.

• The fourth phase oscillates between two extremes (as Chapter 8 demonstrated). On the one hand, the business model might be taking up too much space and overshadow the community model. As the company grows, its product or service offer diversifies to reach targets who are totally extraneous to the community. This may cause community disaffection because the members no longer have good reason to defend an offer that they deem overly commercial. On the other hand, to maintain itself the business needs the authenticity and legitimacy that the existence of the community confers upon its offerings – culminating in the business investing (or reinvesting) the community dimension.

Of course, the entire process requires a mapping of reality to elucidate possible evolutions in community and business model combinations. Reality is much less linear and more chaotic.

THE JUNCTION BETWEEN THE TWO MODELS AND THE SOCIAL VALUE PROPOSITION

The Couchsurfing case study already addressed this point, namely the fact that one of the main hurdles when combining community and business models is the transition between the launch of a movement that has a community flavour and the establishment of an entrepreneurial form. Somewhat more positive examples include the approach that Anthony Vendrame, together with Simon Dubois, took in May 2021 when launching the content agency, 'Crayation', which relied on the Poches&Fils brand (and the strength of the community associated with it) to launch several new businesses. Crayation may have adopted an offbeat and humorous tone in its communications but it is very serious about its goal of helping Quebec entrepreneurs and supporting the region's wider values. The same applies to Anicet Nemani, working through the BIMSTR Agency to promote Cameroonian music or to Gaspard Guermon-prez, who used his FLICK Agency to defend French student interests. Timing and momentum are important as seen in Chapter 8. If the pre-entrepreneurial community period lasts too long, as was the case with Couchsurfing, the risk is that the community will reject the venture's desired 'company with a mission' status.

In short, as desirable as it is to combine the two models, this can be difficult to achieve. The junction between the two models can only really occur if the community model's aims are tied to the business model's value proposition, that is, if the objectives achieved by defending the cause advocated by the community movement aligns with the way the company's offering creates value. This can only happen if there is a broad vision of the company's value creation. Above and beyond economic value, social value – including linking value – becomes paramount.

Many entrepreneurs fail to either grasp this notion or integrate it into their business model. Hence the proposition that the following classification be used to differentiate the three fields of social value creation[8]:

- External social value (or the things that create value for the whole of civil society, namely the social value produced by the activities in which the company engages when defending a movement extraneous to the scope of its sector's activities because it wants to develop connectivity, solidarity initiatives or defend public causes that advance the general interest).

- Internal–external social value (or the social value at the intersection of these two fields, that is, the things that generate

value for employees and customers through their interactions).
Do the products and services on offer speak to customers'
actual interests? Do they enhance a sense of solidarity? Do they
ultimately help to strengthen and consolidate the quality of the
connections that employees are making with customers and/or
customers with one another?

- Internal social value (or the things valued by company's employees). Is it a good place to work? Do people get greater recognition
there than they would elsewhere? Does an above-average climate
of trust and cooperation reign between employees?

Companies do not transfer social value, and in particular they
do not transfer linking value. At most they can define a social value
proposition for their brand or products but this only exists insofar
as people have themselves generated value through their collective
experiences. Social value actually materializes in members' interactions with one another, as demonstrated by the SoulCycle and Tough
Mudder examples. It is co-constructed by community members who
are themselves customers, volunteers and employees all involved in
interactions. They are the people who build social value based on
their exchanges and the things that bring them closer together.

How volunteers are managed clearly also plays a major role in
a project's success. It is a powerful source and driver of innovation but something that is also hard to manage or pilot. Hence the
importance of identifying what motivates volunteers and ensuring
that they share a common vision. It is also necessary that they be
provided from the very outset with direct counterparts; that community managers be empowered to help run operations and that
the (disinterested) community receive material resources along
with opportunities to test ideas they conceptualize together and
which they can then integrate successfully into their work rhythms.

One essential aspect of these new community-centred entrepreneurial approaches is a blurring between what constitutes
voluntary activities (rooted in participants' contributions and
passions) and what constitutes work in the sense of participants'
supervision, organization, validation and instrumentalization. Just
because people may not feel exploited does not mean that brand
volunteers are not being exploited. It is worth remembering that

instrumentalization presupposes a conversion of community involvement into market value but without volunteers questioning their role or place in the process – a frequent occurrence when a venture starts. As the business becomes profitable, a feeling of being exploited is likely to creep in and spread. Entrepreneurs must therefore anticipate and avoid conflict with their volunteers. Relationships must be based on real bonds and on a desire to share something bigger than oneself.

Lastly, to fill in any gaps that might arise as a business matures – and above all, to surround it with people capable of helping it to progress – entrepreneurs must also think about building relationships with stakeholders other than customers, volunteers or (future) employees. Moreover, it is at this level that they take the full measure of linking value, which builds up gradually and must constantly be reviewed, at least tacitly, if only because it calls upon all of the stakeholders comprising the entrepreneurial ecosystem (including suppliers, partners, subcontractors and the organizations responsible for any training, support or subsidizing functions).

NEW STATUTORY FORMS THAT ARE MORE ADAPTED

Current legislation seems to have responded to the growing number of entrepreneurial ventures that combine social and economic missions. The year 2006 saw the advent of a B Corp (Benefit Corporation) status in the United States, the purpose being to support the emergence of for-profit companies defined by their advanced environmental and social performance. Companies completing the B Impact Assessment (BIA) questionnaire are accepting an external validation of their levels of engagement in relation to five main themes: governance, employees, community, environment and customers. They must change their statutes of incorporation to register as B Corps, the idea being this will ensure the permanence of their commitment to make social and environmental considerations central to all operations and decision-making.

One example is a small Montreal company called Snowball that gained B Corp status in 2021 in recognition of its $10 donations to charitable organizations for each purchase made on its platform.

Similarly, Oé, a French website selling organic, vegan and pesticide-free wines, has also received B Corp accreditation.[9] Oé follows a set of processes that advance biodiversity and respect the environment, including natural cork stoppers, recycled paper labels, water-soluble glue, minimized cardboard packaging and above all returnable bottles. Another example is given by Sézane, the women's fashion brand created by Morgane Sézalory that gained the B Corp status in 2021.[10] This new generation of companies pursues statutory social and/or environmental goals in addition to their profit motives, thereby becoming part of a movement of entrepreneurial activists.

Other countries have introduced similar corporate forms, exemplified by France's 'company with a mission' status. To be recognized as such, five conditions must be met:

- a *raison d'être* must be inscribed within the company's statutes of incorporation;

- the same statutes must also specify the social and environmental objectives that the company has set itself the task of pursuing;

- similarly, mission monitoring modalities must also be registered;

- an independent third party must sign off biannual mission fulfilment verifications; and

- the 'company with a mission' description must be registered on the official document attesting to the company's legal existence.

In sum, the new entrepreneurial form comprised start-ups whose entire development rooted in their community base creates an opportunity to rethink, revise and enrich both the management tools that are available to entrepreneurs and the criteria that they use to evaluate start-up possibilities. The usual criteria for success are not only relative in nature but also quite limited, in all likelihood, given the fact that few (if any) take the community strength factor into consideration. As for the feasibility of being successful in the absence of societal, environmental or governance considerations, the reality is that both Millennials and Generation Zs want to work for groups advocating authentic values; create events where people experiment with their freedom and satisfy their search for meaning. The debate about the revolution in work had been going on for several decades now but has further intensified since the Covid-19 crisis erupted. Big companies and start-ups alike are finding it hard to acquire and retain talent, and more broadly, to ensure their communities' adhesion. Entrepreneurial success is no longer being correctly represented in either the media (where everyone imitates everyone else talking about the same competitions or fundraising action) or in the myth of hypergrowth. From a societal perspective, social impact is just as important – if not more so – than economic value. This is the spirit that drives today's start-ups built around communities – and the movement to which they belong.

Renewed entrepreneurial support, both online and face to face, is something that communities also want to see. Support from this corner must get better at incorporating the communal dimension and wedding this to the organizations/ecosystems that sustain entrepreneurship. Indeed, the question must be asked whether it would be better to limit such support to those business founders who have already created communities around a given cause – if only because in that case, support would necessarily be focused on the junction between community and business.

Some may argue that behind a veil of moral sentiments, this book is simply suggesting that business processes be cloaked in a communitarian veil, and that this would create a situation in which connectivity is used to serve material interests rather than the other way around. Were this true, it would belie the aspirations of the authors who – perhaps naively – believe that communities and businesses can be combined without betraying the former (or its constituent emotions and membership connections). Indeed, there are many instances where it is the members of a community who were the main drivers behind the creation of a company that was then meant to serve that community. Of course, it remains essential that these very same members ensure that the newly created company retains its identity and original linking value proposition.

NOTES

1. Alexander Osterwalder & Yves Pigneur, *Business Model Generation: A Handbook for Visionaries, Game Changers, and Challengers*, Chichester: John Wiley & Sons, 2010.

2. https://www.strategyzer.com

3. Alexander Osterwalder, Yves Pigneur, Greg Bernarda, & Alan Smith, *Value Proposition Design: How To Create Products and Services Customers Want*, Chichester: John Wiley & Sons, 2015.

4. Eric Ries, *The Lean Start-up: How Today's Entrepreneurs Use Continuous Innovation to Create Radically Successful Businesses*, New York, NY: Crown Business, 2011.

5. Lean thinking involves the search for a rapid and continuous improvement in an organization's operational efficiency to better meet customer expectations, without having to undertake any major investments or incur additional costs.

6. https://community-canvas.org/

7. https://techcommunity.microsoft.com/t5/yammer-blog/how-to-create-a-sustainable-yammer-community/ba-p/1061527

8. Alain Caillé & Juliette Wéber. "Rendre tangible l'idéal mutualiste par un indicateur de création de valeur sociale." *Revue Internationale de l'Économie Sociale: Recma* 335, 70–85, 2015.

9. https://oeforgood.com/blogs/news/oe-nous-sommes-recertifies-b-corp

10. https://fr.fashionnetwork.com/news/Sezane-avec-la-certification-b-corp-morgane-sezalory-veut-s-affirmer-en-leader-du-renouveau-du-secteur,1353625.html